Estonian Animation:
Between Genius and Utter Illiteracy

To Tom McSorley
For showing me the rink and putting me on the ice

Estonian Animation:
Between Genius and Utter Illiteracy

By Chris Robinson

British Library Cataloguing in Publication Data

Estonian Animation: Between Genius and Utter Illiteracy
A catalogue entry for this book is available from the British Library

ISBN: 0 86196 667 8 (Paperback)

This book was first published as *Between Genius & Utter Illiteracy: A Story of Estonian Animation* (Varrak, 2003). The Estonian Animation Association has granted full rights to John Libbey Publishing for this revised edtion.

Published by
John Libbey Publishing, Box 276, Eastleigh SO50 5YS, UK
e-mail: libbeyj@asianet.co.th; web site: www.johnlibbey.com

Orders: **Book Representation & Distribution Ltd**. info@bookreps.com

Distributed in North America by **Indiana University Press**, 601 North Morton St, Bloomington, IN 47404, USA. www.iupress.indiana.edu

Distributed in Australasia by **Elsevier Australia**, 30–52 Smidmore Street, Marrickville NSW 2204, Australia. www.elsevier.com.au

Distributed in Japan by **United Publishers Services Ltd**, 1-32-5 Higashi-shinagawa, Shinagawa-ku, Tokyo 140-0002, Japan. info@ups.co.jp

Contents

Preface

Pedantic "history" prose

It is not only astonishing that a country like Estonia, with a population of only 1.4 million (of which 1 million are native Estonians), has created very unique and challenging animation over the past thirty years, but also that it has been accomplished in a short time frame under often hostile circumstances. Led by the likes of Priit Pärn, Mati Kütt, Rein Raamat and Elbert Tuganov, Estonian animation can be characterized by its strange combination of the rational and absurd. While the work varies from animator to animator, there is an underlying philosophical, political and ethical nature to the films, which examines how individual identity is affected by shifting ideological structures. In the world of Estonian animation there is no good or bad, no black or white, no single truth. Instead, we find, as Heraclitus once said, "combinations, wholes and not wholes, concurring differing, concordant discordant, from all things one and from one all things." Oh and hey, before you run off in fear of DARK EASTERN EUROPEAN ANGST, let me tell you, many of these films and filmmakers are damn funny, not in a Benny Hill manner, but more in a Monty Python-Marcel Duchamp-Hugo Ball vein.

It was recently discovered that Estonian animation dates back to the early 1930s and a film entitled *Kutsu Juku seiklused* (The Adventures of Juku The Dog, 1931). However, the first Estonian animation studio, Nukufilm, a division of the State's live-action studio Tallinna Kinostuudio, was not created until 1957. Headed by Elbert Tuganov and Heino Pars, Nukufilm's early films, all puppet or cut-out animations, were aimed primarily at children, but as the films grew more satirical and at times poetic, the studio's output eventually became more tailored to an adult audience. In the 1960s, Kalju Kurepõld and Ants Looman made the first drawn animation films for the Soviet Newsreel, Futile (Fuse), followed by commercials for Eesti Reklaamfilm (Estonian Advertising-film). Shortly thereafter Ants Kivirähk and Jaak Palmse made animation telefilms for Estonian Television, and Rein Raamat, a classically trained artist who had worked as a designer with Tuganov, teamed up with Russian animator Fedor Chitruk to establish a cel animation division, Joonisfilm, within Tallinnfilm (formerly Tallinna Kinostuudio).

Under the direction of Raamat and Avo Paistik, Joonisfilm produced ambitious, philosophical films, of which many were based on Estonian folklore. During this period a number of artists emerged from Joonisfilm, most notably Priit Pärn, a former ecologist. In direct contrast to the very traditional and heavily symbol-prone works of earlier animators, Pärn, was influenced by black, absurd humour and the strong caricature tradition in Estonia. Pärn's success and influence led to the development of a new generation of artists with backgrounds not in classical arts, but in political cartoons and surrealism: Mati Kütt, Janno Põldma, Heiki Ernits, Rao Heidmets, and later, Kalju Kivi, Hardi Volmer and Riho Unt.

While Pärn's success as a film director signalled a new era in Estonian animation, it was the convergence of a variety of cultural, political, and geographical factors that made this shift possible. The art scene in Estonia, thanks in part to the 'Khrushchev thaw', changed dramatically during the late 1950s and well into the 1960s and 1970s. Avant-garde ideas gained wider significance and international art began to filter through to Estonia. Translations of classic Western literature by the likes of Samuel Beckett, Franz Kafka, Luigi Pirandello, and Bertold Brecht became available in 1957. In music, numerous cultural exchange programs with the West were set up. All of this led to increased contact with Western artists and an influx of new artistic thinking.

This development was also made possible by Estonia's unique geographical position as an intersection of Western and Eastern cultures. Owing to Estonia's close proximity to Finland, access to Western culture (through Finnish television) was more readily available than for other republics in the Soviet Union, while Estonia's distance from Moscow made it virtually impossible to completely contain nationalist tendencies. Therefore, Estonia was able to get away with a lot more than other republics. In fact, by the mid-1980s and Glasnost, Soviet funding remained strong, but censorship had eased up. At the same time, as evidenced by the increasing number of public protests taking place, the desire for autonomy in Estonia was becoming stronger than ever. For Priit Pärn, this was one of the richest periods for Estonian animation; he fondly refers to it as the 'golden age'.

Ironically, this 'golden age' ended with Estonian independence in

1991. With 'freedom' went both Moscow and funding. Both animation divisions of Tallinnfilm were closed in 1991 and resumed operations under their respective banners: Nukufilm and Eesti Joonisfilm. These studios, owned by the animators, now relied on smaller state grants from the Estonian government and were forced to negotiate a place in the global marketplace to survive. While this dramatic shift has virtually destroyed independent animation in many former Communist countries, the transition to a capitalist marketplace has been relatively smooth for Estonian animators who continue to make their unique and personal films. Of course, the future remains uncertain. Funding could stop tomorrow, forcing the studios to seek industrial support. Additionally, there are new studios (A Film Estonia, Multifilm) competing for the already small pot of available funding. For now, Estonian animation, like the country itself, moves on, however awkwardly.

This book combines interviews with various Estonian animators, critics, and producers, analysis of a variety of films, and introductions to prominent animators, all placed within the backdrop of their respective historical and cultural frameworks.

While we could argue endlessly about the merits of a specific film or filmmaker, what undeniably calls for examination is the historically important uniqueness of this nation. Since the fall of the Iron Curtain, state studios have collapsed everywhere. This has been reflected in the decrease of quality films shown at festival competitions over the last decade. Remarkably, Estonian animation has not only continued to receive state backing, but it has maintained a high level of quality while remaining personal and innovative. Of course, this could all end tomorrow; so all the more reason for us to savour this rigorous and rewarding body of work.

Personal history prose

Ok, now that I've got all that pedantic prose out of the way, let's be clear about one thing: this book does not pretend to be an objective history of Estonia or Estonian animation. This is my take. I've tried to cover all the bases, but I obviously have my own tastes and beliefs. My history with Estonia is professional, but also deeply personal. Many of the animators are my friends. There are many fond moments between us. I cannot, in fact, I will not push those feelings aside. To do so would be false. This does not mean that I will digress into memories of drunken evenings or brothel visits. No, it means that many of these words are laced with an intimacy and awareness that the professional historian might not possess. You've been warned.

"Why Estonia?" You cannot imagine how many times I've heard that bewildered, face-scrunching response when I told someone I was writing this book. I guess it's a good question and ideally this book will serve as its answer.

I first encountered Estonian animation at the Stuttgart Animation Festival in 1996. I was seated comfortably in the upper balcony with a newfound Scottish friend and some cans of some so-so German beer. The first film in competition looked interesting. It was a history of cinema. I had just graduated from Film Studies and was, naturally, interested. The screen went bright white and I saw the line "The cinema it is a lie" come on the screen. An unusual start, I thought. The film continued and before I knew it I was upright for the next thirty minutes, utterly flabbergasted by what I saw before me. The film had this rough, unpolished design style, and a character that looked like a poor imitation of Mr. Potato Head. Then came more stranger characters ... a radish, a carrot ... and all sorts of crazy, grotesque caricatures. Meanwhile, text flew across the screen at a crazy pace, accompanied by an equally hectic soundtrack just as hectic a soundtrack of dialogue. It was breathtaking. I had no idea what the film was about, but I knew I loved its strangeness, intelligence and, most of all, wit.

Sometime that week, maybe after the screening, my friend, Otto Alder, introduced me to the two men who made the film, Janno Põldma and Priit Pärn. They invited Otto and I to their room where we had, I think, some Viru Valge (Estonian vodka). I told them, with 'aw-shucks' schoolboy awe, how much I loved the film. They offered me a cel from the film, which to me was gold, pure GOLD. We maybe had some more drinks and then I said, 'see ya'. The next night (I'll spare the details) the four of us had what remains one of the fondest social evenings of my, then, young life. Unwittingly, this was the beginning of friendships that have lasted to this day.

Later in 1996, I asked my Dutch friend, Gerben Schermer, to organize a screening of Pärn's work at the Ottawa 96 International Animation Festival. Then followed a major Estonian Animation retrospective at Ottawa 98. In the intervening years I had visited Tallinn, Parnu and Tartu, screened many films, met almost every animator and gathered more than enough information to mount the retrospective and write the complementary article that appeared in the festival catalogue. Four programmes of Estonian Animation were presented at Ottawa 98, as well as an exhibition of Mati Kütt's animation art. Pärn, Põldma, Kütt, Olav Ehala and Rao Heidmets were all guest attendees too. And, although no one believes me, it was also at this very same festival that Priit Pärn won, without my influence, the Grand Prize for his film, *The Night of the Carrots.*

Why was I so hooked? Maybe I saw a similarity between Canada and Estonia. Both are rooted in peasantry; both share superpowers as neighbours. Is it coincidental that one of the largest Estonian populations abroad is in Canada? Perhaps that's a lot of cow chew. Maybe the work just matched my temperament at of the time. I liked smart, bizarre humour. Maybe I felt superior to the 'morons' who didn't 'get it', who couldn't understand the humour, and who only saw half-worn clichés about KGB symbolism. Perhaps it was the case of a fresh-faced, deeply shy festival director of little experience seeking to find a niche, to find something that set him apart. Or maybe this Estonian fascination was all just rooted in a need to find myself. Hell, maybe I just needed an excuse to drink Viru Valge.

Me and you aside, the Estonia story is an underdog's story. Estonians may not like to hear that, but hey, it's a reality. Estonia has a small population, relatively few people speak the native language, and yet it has not only survived, but survived well. Estonia has remained rooted to its cultural traditions despite the sweeping sameness of corporate-injected culture.

Chris Robinson
Ottawa, Canada
Revised edition, July 2006

Acknowledgements

This book is a culmination of six years of exposure to everything Estonia. I express infinite thanks to Priit Pärn and Janno Põldma, who not only supported this project and encouraged the Estonian Film Foundation and Estonian Cultural Endowment to do so too, but made the film that got me hooked in the first place. Beyond that, they have been damn fine friends.

Otto Alder and Gerben Schermer. My brothers. They not only guided me on my Estonian adventures, but also through the world of animation and through life when I was but a young, naïve punk who thought he knew it all.

Jaak Lõhmus and Riina Sildos at the Estonian Film Foundation for having faith in a non-Estonian. Additionally, I'd also like to thank Jaak whose research effectively became the section, *The Lost Film*.

Rao Heidmets and Mati Kütt have always opened their lives and doors to me without hesitation. Our relationships have always felt natural to me, like those of (functional) family.

David Ehrlich for being such a patient and caring friend and for constantly challenging my many spouts of doubt.

Arko Okk, Tiina Märtens and Ly Pulk whose assistance and support during the two weeks that Otto Alder and I spent researching in Tallinn in March 2002 were kindly appreciated.

Pearu Tamberg at the Estonian Film Archives for access to many films, videos, and photographs.

Closer to home, I thank my Estonian language teacher, Enel Onu, and Illimar and Tiiu Altosaar, Sulev Rooster (Estonian Embassy in Ottawa) and Ave Kalmus for generously interpreting and translating some materials.

And naturally, I thank all the people who contributed in some form or another to the making of this book: Priit Tender, Ülo Pikkov, Jaan Ruus, Olav Ehala, Sven Grünberg, Hardi Volmer, Riho Unt, Arvo Nuut, Heiki Ernits, Mikk Rand, Rein Raamat, Avo Paistik, Aarne Ahi, Jüri Arrak, Leonard Lapin, Elbert Tuganov, Heino Pars, Kalju Kurepõld, Kalev Tamm, Peep Pedmanson, Kasper Jancis, Ants Looman, Kaie Pärn, Kalju Kivi, Andrus Kivirähk, Timo Viljakainen, Margareta Nygard, Edwin Carels, Grant Chang, Tina Paas, Paul Fierlinger, Alyson Carty, Karlo Funk, Dave Dyment, Igor Kovalyov, Heather Kenyon, Maureen Furniss, Richard Meltzer, Barry Doyle, Lauren Donen, Chris Weissbach, and the guy who socked me in the stomach at Lilys 'bar' in Tallinn.

And now, the honour roll ...

Mait Laas is extraordinary. He put up with my endless queries via email, found books for me, interviewed Elbert Tuganov and Heino Pars on my behalf, and filled in so many of the little gaps that I'd stepped over. He is also a fine human being.

Dennis Sabourin and Genevieve Willis for proofing and editing my often lazy and barely literate scribblings.

Peeter Tammisto went beyond the call of duty translating a variety of texts, chasing people down for interviews, and even reading books for me. And hey, he's Canadian too!

And ... huff ... huff ... huff ... finally, I thank Kelly Neall, Jarvis Robinson Neall and Betty Neall for their patience and seemingly indestructible love.

Chapter One

Previous Attractions

To see what is, we must see what was. I've no intention of going into Estonian history in great detail as there are already two fine books in English on the subject: Rein Taagerpera's *Estonia: Return To Independence* and Toivo Raun's *Estonia and The Estonians*. However, it is important to highlight a few characteristics of Estonian history in order to better contextualize this story.

In the beginning was land, and then came the word to deem it land. This particular land was located snugly between the Gulf of Finland, Lake Peipsi, Latvia and the Baltic Sea. This land, known by a variety of names including Kunda, Livonia, and Estonia (Eesti), became a corridor between the West and the East. Because of this enviable geographical location, Estonia has been a desirable target for many empires since the 13th century. Since about 1227, Estonia has been under the rule of Denmark, Poland, and most influentially, Sweden (1561–1710), Germany (1227–1561, 1941–45) and Russia (1710–1860, 1945–1991). There have only been three periods when Estonia was an independent country: 1200A.D., 1918–1940 and 1991–present.

Given its small population and relatively small land size (noteworthy though, Estonia is bigger than The Netherlands), by all rights, Estonia should not exist today. The reason it does exist says a lot about the character of the people, but also the language they speak.

I've read various attempts that try to define the essence of an Estonian, and honestly they're ludicrous. I've read of Estonians' calmness, ironic sense of humour, pride, and sincerity, and while I've certainly encountered these traits, I've also seen their polar opposites. I've seen the good and the bad, just as I see it everyday in my own city. Furthermore, to speak of some homogeneity of race is misleading. Today, one can see traces of Swedish, German, and Russian, while emerging more recently is the influence of

'American' culture throughout Estonia. Estonians were once forced to speak Russian; now they are 'forced' to speak English. Certainly the reasons are entirely different – one was a gun to the head, the other is the enticing dollar bill. What has saved and made Estonians distinct, is their language.

North American English has swept across the planet forcing virtually every culture that wishes to participate in a global economy to embrace the language of Americans. I need not go into a long diatribe about the dangers of this global assimilation – if not perpetuated by the Americans, then it'd be by someone else. Nevertheless, along the way, we (English-speaking North Americans) have become spoiled modernists, racing through time crippled by historical amnesia. We now not only assume that everyone can and should speak English, but that they quite likely think like us as well (whoever 'us' is!). As 'we' invade every part of the world with our language and 'culture' we are not only forcing other languages to the background, but also the subconscious aspects of those languages that truly define the essence of difference. I speak of gestures, tone and pace. When we think, we think through language. Language influences how we perceive the world. In the Estonian language, gender does not exist. In place of pronouns, there are about 14 noun/adjective/pronoun and numeral cases. No definite or indefinite articles exist. And, most difficult, at least for me, is the three-quantity system (which might have North German roots) in vowels and consonants. For example, the short vowel: *sada* means "hundred", long vowel: *saada!* means "send!" and the very long vowel: *saada* means "to receive". In short, the Estonian language is drastically different from the more common Indo-European languages. With that difference comes a different way of thinking and seeing the world.

The Estonian language can be traced back some 5000 years. It is part of the Finno-Ugric group. Currently, aside from a part of the Volga region, Hungary, Finland and Estonia are the sole inheritors of this language group, with Finland aligned to the Finno branch, Hungary the Ugric, and Estonia a subgroup of the Finno branch, Balto-Finnic.

Today there are about 1million people who speak Estonian around the world. It's almost like a secret society and there is little doubt that the uniqueness of the Estonian language is at the root of Estonia's survival. The language is so complex for foreigners that assimilating or eradicating Estonian culture was made all the more difficult for invaders. Ironically, many of Estonia's occupants had to learn Estonian to communicate their commands. Sure you could shoot everyone, but then who'd clean the dishes?

The Estonian language and character is deeply rooted in the land. In fact, some of the earliest known Estonian words like *mägi* (hill) and *mets* (forest) are still in usage today. So Estonians might often be using words whose origins date back some 5000 years. Given the age of both the language and the land, there is a sense of stability or permanence found in Estonia that appears to be absent in, for example, North America, where the land is massive, relatively young, and continually abused. When islands comprise 10 per cent of a country that is already 44 per cent forest and 22 per cent wetland, it's a given that landscape is closely bound up with the language and the people.

Not altogether surprisingly, animism was the predominant belief of early Estonians. Trees, stones, land, rivers, and even fire were believed to possess spirits. Unconvinced? Then just take a look at the meanings of the names of many of the Estonian animators: Pärn (close to lime, as in lime tree), Põldma (of the field), Kütt (hunter), Kalju (rock), Kivi (stone), Rand (Shore or coast), and Raamat (book).

Culture

While Estonia's position as a 'bridge' between East and West led to centuries of occupation and bloodshed, it also had positive repercussions – namely a strange combination of isolation and openness. The isolation has helped Estonia preserve its roots and yet the diversity of its neighbours has meant an exposure to a wide range of cultural influences.

Prior to the 19th century, a strong oral tradition through folk songs prevailed in Estonia, in particular by the *regivärss* folk song, which used a lot of alliteration and thematic repetition (myths, weddings, daily life). The first written evidence of Estonian language appeared in the 13th century. Ironically, most of the early writings were published by foreigners keen on converting the pagan Estonians into God-fearing Christians. The first all-Estonian language book was published in 1535. The first known work written by an Estonian was Käsu Hans' 1708 poem lamenting the destruction of Tartu (by Russians, naturally) during the Great Northern War (1700–21).

Formal education dates back to the 1600s. Most significantly, although Estonian was not initially taught at the school, Swedish rulers founded Tartu University in 1632. The University was closed in 1710 and re-opened in 1802. It continues to be Estonia's most prestigious school.

It wasn't until the 19th century that Estonian culture really took off (as it did in many European countries where Empires had started to collapse). This cultural period, most active from 1860–1885, is generally referred to as the National Awakening. In just three decades, Estonia became a nation with a weekly newspaper, books (including the publication of the National epic, *Kalevipoeg,* written by F.R. Kreutzwald), poetry, literary societies, theatre groups (the first Estonian play was written by Lydia Koidula, who was also Estonia's first important poet), choirs, orchestras and, most significantly, song festivals. The first song festival was held in Tartu in 1869. There were about 900 participants and an audience of some 10–15,000. While Estonian music was not a major part of this first festival, the symbolic and literal importance of the event cannot be overlooked. Here were thousands of people singing about Estonians for Estonians. The energy from both the songs and the intimate gathering must have been overwhelming, and certainly stimulated a sense of togetherness and national pride in Estonians.

Cultural expression was not only a way of communicating with one another, but was also an essential means of self-preservation. During Soviet occupation, for example, a song festival provided a subtle and effective method of Estonian resistance. It was the one moment when Estonians gathered together and were able, albeit modestly, to express their world in their own voices. The song festival provided hope for the future and served as an important bridge to the past. Little wonder, then, that Estonia's exit from the Soviet Union was deemed The Singing Revolution.

Chapter Two

The Lost Film

Because of World War 1 and the War of Independence, Estonian cinema did not develop until the 1920s. However, in 1916, prior to the first independence, a photographer named Johannes Pääsuke became a pioneer with the short film *Karujaht Pärnumaal* (Bear Hunt in Pärnumaa), a satire about the stupidity of city bureaucrats. Estonian cinema's first feature film was Konstantin Märska's *Mineviku varjud* (Shadows of the Past, 1924), which, either lost or destroyed, has not survived.

Like the films of almost every other country at the time, Estonian films were naïve and exaggerated. There were good guys and bad guys, gals needing to be rescued, lowered brows, and eye-rolling – the usual fare, just like every other national cinema. Aside from the occasional fictional film, there were many media-related films covering a wide range of domestic topics or showcasing local celebrities and politicians. There were also educational films showing viewers how to bind books, make crochet patterns, and even farms bees farm.

None of the filmmakers were professional. They received state support and, so it appears, made movies less out of a desire for financial gain (although there were some small businessmen involved, perhaps believing they could re-coup an investment) than a technical and artistic fascination with this new medium. But the period of experimentation was short-lived. A limited marketplace, the arrival of sound, and, with that, bigger budgets effectively killed off the first chapter of Estonian cinema.

In 1936, the Estonian government established Estonian Culture Film (although it was actually founded in 1931). The aim of the organization was not unlike that of the National Film Board of Canada (founded in 1939): to showcase what was perceived to be the nation's life, culture and values. In short, Estonian Culture Film was a propaganda unit designed to flaunt the nation's achievements, so its filmic output was mostly of the newsreel variety. Each cinema was obliged to show an Estonian newsreel before the main feature. The main features were generally what filmgoers of other nations saw: Hollywood, French, German, and British feature films. And what of Estonian features? The focus on short documentary newsreels left little money for expensive sound pictures.

Until 1986, it was assumed that animation was not among the many early cinematic experiments. It was always thought that Elbert Tuganov's *Little Peter's Dream* (1957) was Estonia's first animation film. However, a roll of film was found in what was then the State Central Archives of the History of the Estonian Soviet Socialist Republic. The piece of film was discovered, oddly enough, in the section dedicated to the Estonian Temperance Society and turned out to be a cut-out animation film entitled *The Adventures of Juku the Dog,* whose main character is a puppy with long, floppy ears. The silent piece is awkward and sloppy in places, but an overall adequate emulation of 1930s-era American animation.

Juku appears to have been an attempt to create an Estonian national icon of the likes of Mickey Mouse. The making of *Juku* was also meant to jumpstart Estonia's entrance into animation. As Nool, the society paper, noted in an article dated 1 May 1931, "This film is an endeavour to enter into the field where only big film countries, such as Germany and the United States have worked. Despite technical difficulties we tried to do our best to win the hearts of all Estonian film-lovers."

Juku was the creation of at least three men: Voldermar Pats (photography), Elmar Janimagi (drawings), and Alexander Teppor. Teppor, a noted portrait photographer, was among those trying to establish an Estonian film industry in the early 1920s. Teppor often photographed on-set goings-on during filming and his photo studio served as a meeting place for film people. Pats, the nephew of Estonian President Konstantin Pats, had already served as the cinematographer on many feature films during the 1920s and Janimagi was a noted caricaturist (referred to as Jani in the film's credits). For Janimagi this was the first and last animation film to which he would contribute. He was murdered in 1932.

Originally intending to make a series of films, the trio had not foreseen the numerous difficulties they'd encounter with their first:

> Much had to be learned and discovered in this comparatively unfamiliar field of filming. This is why the new film has to be regarded as experimental. At first, when the landscape was drawn on ordinary paper, it started bouncing, as it is impossible to produce an identical landscape on so many

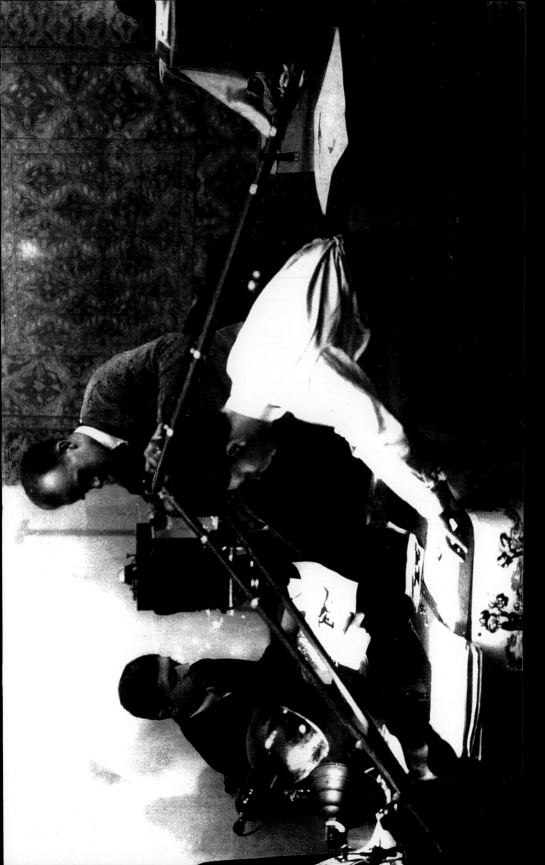

drawings. This drawing was covered with transparent paper onto which the moving images were drawn. The film with a length of approximately 180 metres needed nearly 5000 individual drawings.

Frame from the film *Kutsu Juku*.

Interestingly, archivists only found 100 metres of the film, meaning that 80 metres are lost to the dustbin of history.

The film was to première, according to newspapers, on 7 November 1931, along with a feature film called *Atlantis: Kalmistu Mere Sügavuses* (Atlantis: The Graveyard in the Depth of the Sea), which was being promoted as the first "light and sound" film shown in Estonia. As for the newspaper's billing of the other "great film":

> "Novelty! The First Estonian animated trick film, a sound grotesque *"Juku the Dog"*.

The premiere took place at the Capitol Cinema, which had recently installed "modern sound equipment." But, as *Juku* was shot silent, its soundtrack was to be provided by "records of the Tormolen Co. Parlophon", cued to play while the film unspooled.

Little is known of the film's reception, or even if it was shown. Teppor's daughter does remember that her father, sensitive to the oncoming political turmoil, placed the film in the national archives. At the end of the 1980s, during the restoration of Teppor's home and studio, some glass negatives were found. One of those negatives shows behind the scenes footage of the three men at work on *Juku*.

Following the film's discovery in 1986, *Juku* was shown on Estonian Television. In 1996 it was restored in Finland with a new soundtrack. And in 2001, Estonia suddenly found itself celebrating the 70th anniversary of animation production.

In an article from which I've borrowed heavily for this entire chapter, Jaak Lõhmus notes that the caricature influence we see in many later Estonian films was already visible in *Juku*. After all, the contemporary press referred to Juku as a "grotesque". Naturally, influence is a moot point given the film's four decades of silence. Nevertheless, it shows how caricature, absurd humour and a modern sensibility were already present in 1930s Estonia.

As it turns out, *Juku* was not the only animation film work created in the 1930s. "We have information about four animation films Film advertisement. made during the 1930s." says Jaak Lõhmus. While *Juku* was in

Esimese eesti joonis-trikkfilmi valmistajad: kunstnik Elmar Janimägi ja filmioperaator V. Päts.

production, a drawing film was also being made in Tartu, but nothing confirms this. Edmund Martin, who now lives in Long Island, N.Y. with his daughter, was at work on the puppet film called *The Forest Tale,* about two kids who get lost in the forest. The last of the known 1930s animated films of Estonia was called *Kaval Ants and Vanapagan.*

But let's not overexaggerate *Juku*'s importance. Artistically, it is nothing to blink at and there is almost nothing about the film that suggests any connection with later Estonian animations. In fact, if anything, *Juku* is a typically Western product owing more to Walt Disney than to any Estonian roots.

"It is an incidental film," says film critic, Jaan Ruus. "It is a nice little piece but doesn't influence the general development. Estonian cinema in the 1930s was typically European. We saw the same films as everyone else and the discovery just gives us a nice reason to celebrate the birth of Estonian animation ... but Estonian Animation wasn't really born then."

Nevertheless, *Juku* exists and should obviously be acknowledged. And for anyone unfamiliar with Estonia who might think of it as a cold, isolated Eastern European country, *Juku*, among other things, clearly shows the fallacy of such an assumption. In the 1930s, Tallinn was a modern, European-like city with access not only to all sorts of international art and thought, but with entrepreneurial awareness as well. *Juku* was to be the goldmine that made Pats, Janimagi, and Teppor famous, putting Estonia on the cultural map alongside Walt Disney. It didn't quite work out that way, which ain't necessarily a bad thing.

Chapter Three

The Dictator and the Democrat

Ironically, Elbert Tuganov, the grand papa of Estonian animation, was actually born in Baku, Azerbaijan (1920). Just two years later the Islamic country would become one of the Soviet's republics. "Since my grandparents on my father's side were Moslems, they apparently fled from their homeland during the revolution and settled in Azerbaijan because they thought they would be safer there as far as their religion was concerned. My parents were married in 1920."

The Estonian connection came via Tuganov's mother, a Lutheran of Estonian background. Her paternal grandfather was from the Viljandi region of Estonia. He pursued work as a tailor but found there was too much competition in Tallinn so he moved to Helsinki, then to St. Petersburg and finally, after hearing there was oil to be found, went to Baku. There were lots of rich people in Baku and they needed some fine cloth. So Tuganov's great grandfather settled in Baku and voilà … he had a kid. That kid had a kid and that kid in turn begat the boy named Elbert Tuganov.

Life in Baku was short and not so sweet. By 1924, Tuganov's parents had divorced. Tuganov lived with his mother and her big family. But within three years, six of the nine family members breathed their last breaths. The remaining Tuganov clan – Elbert, his mother and grandmother – decided to return to Estonia. The homecoming was momentary. "After three months," says Tuganov, "we moved on to Berlin, where one of my mother's sisters lived. She invited us to live with her. Mother returned to Baku and planned to follow us to Berlin a couple of years later."

Life became, to some degree, stable for Tuganov. He graduated from elementary school in 1931 and then from grammar school

Elbert Tuganov.

in 1939. "I was a young man. We lived decently but we were not very rich. Any young man wants to have some pocket money. I went to work at a Russian restaurant in Berlin and earned very good money there. I waited tables, and I was a tobacco vendor selling cigarettes and cigars from a box that hung from my neck in front of my stomach, and sometimes I worked in the cloakroom. I earned very good money from tips."

Tuganov liked the money, but he didn't like the job. He didn't like bowing to the customers. He didn't like collecting their coats. One day he saw a newspaper ad offering work on animation films. He got the job and so began his animation career. Tuganov worked for two private film studios in Germany. The first was an animation studio that made theatrical commercials and the second was a large film company called Döhring Film. The former was a small studio whose employees numbered about 7–8 people. The studio's owner was the cameraman and his wife was the art director. They hired people when they had commissions and then, like now, laid them off when the work was completed. Tuganov did his work and was let go. After a brief turn at another small studio, Tuganov found work at the large Döhring Film company. "I didn't take these jobs solely for money," says Tuganov. His experience at Döhring was brief but important. There he learned the different phases (in-betweening, transfers) that comprised the creation of an animation film.

When Hitler took power, Tuganov decided it was best to return to Estonia, to perform his military service, planning to later return to Berlin to study his first love, architecture. "I wanted to be an architect from an early age already. My father was a civil engineer and an artist, and he wrote to me. His dream was for me to become a great architect and he would then supervise the construction of my designs. This became my plan at the age of 14–15 but life turned out differently."

This is probably as good a place as any to throw in some historical background. As is well known today, Germany and the USSR signed the Molotov-Ribbentrop Pact in August 1939. The crux of the agreement was that Germany could invade Poland and the USSR could take the Baltic countries. Within a month Stalin moved roughly 160,000 Soviet troops to the Estonian border and demanded that Soviet military bases be established in Estonia. As their army only numbered 16,000 troops, the Estonians had little choice but to succumb. Estonia was coerced into signing a mutual assistance pact with the USSR in September 1939. Within a year, while the world's attention was focussed on Germany's invasion of France, the USSR falsely accused Estonia of violating the pact and of further dubious anti-Soviet plotting. What the USSR demanded of Estonia was unlimited entry of Soviet troops and the formation of a pro-Soviet government. In a bid to legitimate its accusations of Estonian resistance, Moscow even staged a phoney uprising that included members of the Communist Party of Estonia and Soviet civilian workers from nearby military bases posing as local demonstrators. Once this was done, Soviet occupation was relatively fast and smooth. In a few months the Estonian army became part of the Soviet Red Army and Russians or other trustworthy Communists replaced government officials. Peeter Tammisto, a Canadian-Estonian who works for Eesti Joonisfilm, tells a story about his father (who was just a year older than Tuganov) which provides an interesting overall impression of what life was like for young Estonian men during WWII. "My dad started military service at the same time as Tuganov, but was in the armored unit. My dad's unit was pulled back into Russia not far east of Estonia where they were supposed to make a stand against the advancing German Army. My dad was at the lookout post, where he was supposed to direct artillery fire in case of attack. He saw the Germans coming through a rye field, all with tree branches tied to their helmets. They could easily have mowed them all down as the bushes on their helmets made them particularly visible in the rye field. But my dad just watched them come and did not report anything on purpose until it was too late. The Germans overran their position and practically everybody was taken prisoner. After about half a year as a POW, he was enlisted in the German Army and participated in the battles to defend against the advance of the Red Army in 1944. His unit retreated and was pulled back to Germany and he ended up deployed in Yugoslavia at the end of the war. He was lucky to make it through Czechoslovakia to the West and eventually from there to Canada. That is the story of Tuganov's and my dad's generation. They were both in the Estonian Army, then the Red Army and a different twist of fate could have landed Tuganov on the German side after all, even though he went to lengths to avoid just that."

Upon his return to Estonia, Tuganov enlisted in the cavalry. He had just finished his basic training and was working as a military school instructor in Tallinn when he learned that the Estonian army had been incorporated into the Red Army. His unit was deployed to the town of Tjumen, in Siberia. Since Tuganov had recently returned from Germany, the Soviets considered him suspect and kept him from front line duty. He was relegated to a reserve unit. Tuganov's term of service in the Red Army ended when he was discharged on 1 January 1946.

Tuganov's dream to study architecture in Germany was no longer an option.

After his discharge, Tuganov sought employment at Tallinnfilm (the state film studio). He was offered a cameraman's assistant position in their "so-called animation department." For eleven years, Tuganov shot, drew, and painted titles and credit sequences. During this time he also modernized the studio's primitive technical apparatus. "Originally," says Tuganov, "they used to nail the credits to the wall and the camera was set up on a tripod." So, in order to shoot credits more adequately and fashion trick shots, Tuganov built an animation stand that would allow the studio to do frame by frame shooting. A visiting Moscow official was impressed by the new apparatus and suggested that the studio make animation films.

Tuganov immediately set out to find scripts and stories that would be suitable for production. He landed a Danish story called *Palle Alone in the World* . This became the basis for the first Nukufilm production, *Peetrikese unenagu* (Little Peter's Dream, 1957). "The main reason we chose it," says Tuganov, "was because it had one character." It was an experimental work and was financed using the studio's own money; Moscow provided no funding and so had no editorial control. Tuganov bought the book, wrote the script and, as no one else at the studio knew anything about animation films, did all the pre-production.

Once Tuganov had completed the script, he presented it to the studio's board of directors who, in turn, presented it to the Ministry of Education of the Estonian Soviet Republic. It was a nerve-wracking wait for Tuganov, and the response from the officials was not positive. "The response," notes Tuganov, "was that this kind of story cannot be accepted because every good Soviet child rises properly in the morning, says 'good morning' to his parents, washes himself, eats breakfast, and only then can he go outside. Our director was an intelligent man, though, and he put the film into production at his own risk."

Tuganov deliberately planned *Little Peter's Dream* as a puppet film because he lacked the luxury of time and the necessary personnel to make a drawing film. Seven people worked on *Little Peter's Dream*, including future Joonisfilm studio founder, Rein Raamat, and a young Moscow film school graduate named Aimée Beekmann.

In the film, a troublesome little boy, a playground bully, endures an evening of nightmares in which he wanders through a deserted city. In the end, the boy awakes fearful but with a new awareness of the importance of being kind to others. Consequently, he returns to the playground with a much better attitude.

While *Little Peter's Dream* is aimed at a child audience, the film is

filled with dark and almost hostile scenarios (e.g. Peter crashes a streetcar). At times, Peter's wanderings through the deserted city streets seem more in tune with the existential landscapes of a Samuel Beckett or Buster Keaton work.

With a running time of twenty minutes, *Little Peter's Dream* is far too long and the main character is not interesting enough to hold the audience's attention. Nevertheless, the film is not as primitive as one might expect. The animation is awkward and jumpy at times, but the character rendering and set design are, not surprisingly given Tuganov's architecture aspirations, quite accomplished and original. Even Tuganov is quite frank about his first film: "It was our first experience in shooting, directing and editing animated film. Looking at it now, it is too long and awkward. But it was just our first film."

Incredibly, the film was realised without once consulting Moscow. When the completed film was eventually screened for officials in Moscow, there was initial surprise that an animation film had been made in Tallinn. However, *Little Peter's Dream* was approved and shown in theatres all over the Soviet Union.

After *Little Peter's Dream*, the production of puppet animation continued with two long and dull fairy tales, *Pohjakonn* (Frog, 1959) and *Metsamuinasjutt* (Forest Tale, 1960). The filmmaking process mimicked that of the first production. Six or seven people worked on the film alongside artists from the Estonian puppet theatre. "We ordered the puppets for our first films according to sketches from the puppet theatre," says Tuganov. "The theatre made the puppets for us and then we made the film."

After the fourth film, *Mina ja Murri* (Mina and Murri, 1961), animation production received a budgetary blessing from Tallinnfilm. The division's staff grew to twenty and it was decided that the puppets would then be fashioned in the studio.

Once Tuganov received the permission to keep producing films, he ensured that there would be no gaps in production. "I tried to keep the crew together so that we could make these films in uninterrupted succession. I had worked alone for six years. I wanted to make these films and that is why I kept our group together. Nobody else had worked in animation before, so we had to learn how, and then we made films." This meant that Tuganov was forced to accept stories that he was not so fond of. "I had a crew that I had to provide work for. I was worried that if they had no work, then the studio would be disbanded and then I would not have the opportunity to make animated films when I needed it."

The decision to make animation films for children was influenced to a small degree by the successes of Disney and Soyultzmultfilm studios and quite simply by the fact that Tuganov had a young child at the time. "I made my first films as if I was making them for my own children."

While he was quite careful to avoid making preachy, overly moralistic films, most of Tuganov's films contained some sort of message. "The stories I adapted or made up myself all had some sort of point. I did not like abstract films and I did not know how to make them. I loved humour and at the time I made those films, humour had a very good effect on our everyday work. Films that made people smile were very well received."

One of the first films to achieve critical success was *Ott kosmoses* (Ott in Space, 1961). The story, which echoes that of *Little Peter's Dream,* follows a mischievous little boy named Ott who leaves school, finds himself near a rocket launch site, and then manages to blast off into space inside one of the rockets. While in space, he encounters a variety of strange creatures and planets. After battling off a lion, a giant, and a one-legged creature with a gas mask for a face, the terrified little boy manages to return to earth having learned his lesson of humility.

Like *Little Peter*, *Ott* features some original character design, most notably the scary gas-masked one-legged machine gun-toting creature with a brush standing atop his helmet, and a number of intricate and detailed set designs. The animation remains awkward but is certainly an improvement upon *Little Peter*.

When all was said and done, *Ott* was loved by kids throughout the Soviet Union and was the first Estonian animation film to win an award. But getting that award is a story in itself. "Moscow sent *Ott in Space* to the world's first Astronautics and Aeronautics Film Festival in Donville, France in 1961," says Tuganov. "I didn't know anything about it. Then I read the latest news from the back page of the monthly Russian journal, *Kino,* which said that 'Kot in Space' [meaning Tomcat in Space] earned an award at this festival." The next time Tuganov was in Moscow he asked about the award. "I said the name was Ott not Kot and that it was a Tallinnfilm film." Refused the award, Tuganov decided to pursue his inquiry with the Deputy Minister. "I told him that our studio won some sort of award and you refuse to give it to us. So this is how you collect the awards from all the republics of the USSR and keep them in your own hands and take credit for them. That's not right!" With the Deputy Minister's intervention, Moscow officials finally relented and Tuganov received "a very nice trophy and medal." Today it hangs on the wall in the Nukufilm studio. "In those days," adds Tuganov, "the directors and authors of films had no idea where their films were being sent. Nowadays you are the masters of your own films."

And if getting your due awards was difficult, gaining access to film prints of your own work was even more problematic for filmmakers. "We finished *Ott in Space,*" says Tuganov, "and afterwards we didn't hear anything more about it. But once I wanted to use the print. Boris Kõrver (the composer) asked me to go with him to show the film at a factory in Kehra. They wanted him to arrange a screening for them. I went to a minister in the administration at that time, and made a request on behalf of Kõrver and myself to borrow the print of the film. The minister told me that, 'This film belongs to the state and you cannot have it.' The director and composer could not go in person to show their film to anybody!"

Censorship problems existed but, surprisingly, they originated mostly from Tuganov's own administrators at Tallinnfilm. "It was not so easy. Sometimes they pulled dirty tricks. They made calls to the appropriate authorities in Moscow and told them things, what they thought of certain things." In hindsight the problems were minor, even trivial. *Peaaegue uskumatu lugu* (An Almost Unbelievable Story, 1962) caused a very minor stir when it offended the studio's executive editor. In the film (based on a newspaper article that Tuganov had read), a greedy factory owner replaces his workers with monkeys. The studio's executive editor interpreted this as making fun of the workers. The film was momentarily banned, but once the clever bureaucrats realized that the film ridiculed capitalism, it was released.

During the making of *Talent* (1963), about a young boy being pressured by his father into becoming a person of social standing, a studio administrator named Remmelgas demanded that the boy's father have a definite job, that he clearly be labelled a worker. The demand grew louder when Remmelgas expressed his concern to the new studio editor, Sylvia Kiik. Tuganov, who could be quite obstinate, disagreed with the complaint and, in the end, just ignored his superiors. When Remmelgas and Kiik screened *Talent*, they saw that Tuganov had not paid their concerns any attention. Their response was simply that the father didn't need to have a definite job after all! Tuganov was particularly annoyed that Kiik, who was supposed to represent the interests of the animators, said nothing. "In the event of a conflict, you think and deliberate and deal with the problem in particular. But when one side keeps harping on the same thing, it pisses you off."

Sylvia Kiik, who had joined Tallinnfilm in 1962, is sometimes referred to as the most powerful person in the Estonian animation

studios of the Soviet era. She had come to Talllinnfilm from television. While television was a young, developing media, Kiik deemed the film world a "rather petrified, Russian-minded and Russian language institution, which has no creative atmosphere whatsoever." However, Kiik discovered Nukufilm to be full of life and closely connected with Estonian culture. "Our directors made the puppet films, the specialists were trained during the production process, Estonian writers, artists and composers participated in the creative process."

The editor's job was like that of a "housewife whose work never ended," says Kiik. "The editor had to be a little bit of a producer, a little bit of a lawyer, a little bit of a consultant, critic or curator, and sometimes a scapegoat, whatever was needed."

As with the entire country, the film industry was governed by a planned economy. Productions had to be formulated and budgeted in advance. Kiik designed a yearly plan that included a list of films to be made. Each screenplay had to be submitted to Moscow for approval but it was pretty much a formality in those days because the films were aimed at children. A storyboard was then created and both script and storyboard were sent for approval to the management of the studio. Prior to completion, the director would show Kiik a mute version of the film. If all was deemed acceptable by the artistic commission, then the film was handed over to Goskino where they then ordered screening prints for distribution throughout the Soviet Union.

Kiik answered to eight superiors – the most powerful of whom resided in Moscow. But the responsibility for ensuring the timely production of an acceptable script rested solely with Kiik. "Each of the local superiors had his own wishes and also his own goals," notes Kiik, "it all had to be listened to, get the signature and then forget about it." When productions went smoothly, the studio editor escaped notice. But when problems arose, as in the case of *An Almost Incredible Story*, all involved would turn to the studio editor.

One of the major weaknesses of Nukufilm's early films had more to do with technical censorship than with content conflicts. The Soviet Union dictated a running time of either ten or twenty minutes as a full reel of film comprised ten minutes. A regulation applied throughout the Soviet Union, films could be no longer or shorter. "It was for technical reasons," says Tuganov, "for the sake of the projectionists. I was in Bulgaria once and I saw some wonderful films that were all 2–3 minutes long. Later [around 1969] I made a report stating that not every film should have to be stretched out to ten minutes. Not long after they finally hanged the law."

By 1961, it became clear that Tuganov alone could not maintain enough of a workload to keep everyone employed. He decided to find a second director. Heino Pars worked as a camera assistant to Aimée Beekmann on *Little Peter's Dream* and *A Forest Tale*. When Beekmann left, Pars stepped in and worked as cinematographer for the next eight Nukufilm films.

Heino Pars.

Heino Pars was born in a small town in central Estonia. "Everyone knew each other by appearance," says Pars. "The town had mostly small houses with large yards. The people were very close to the land and to nature, as most of them raised animals. Father was a self-taught gardener and beekeeper, and he also ran a shop, so he worked in many fields of activity. I had one sister and one brother. I was born as a twin but my twin brother died at the age of 2½."

By sixth grade, Pars had developed some interest in the arts. The school's annual Christmas and spring celebrations enabled Pars to perform and direct plays with his fellow students. "I was allowed to stage one sketch in the sixth grade and that made me feel real important." Following elementary school, Pars briefly attended high school in Viljandi, until the Russians and Germans arrived. Pars was drafted into the German army and ended up getting seriously wounded and taken prisoner by the Russians. Evidently, Pars recovered; yet the experience left him with an interest in medicine. "I decided that I wanted to study medicine but since I had not been in school for many years and the competition to be admitted to the faculty of medicine was very stiff, I thought I would try veterinary medicine." Initially, Pars had hoped to transfer to the Faculty of medicine and so looked upon his vet studies as temporary. Pars was right: his veterinarian career would be short-lived, but not for the reasons he had hoped. "I did not complete my studies because the Russians then started mass deportations. My mother was deported to Siberia. Although they left my brother and I alone and we remained in Estonia, I thought they wouldn't let me graduate anyway."

Pars did manage to graduate and soon found work as a part time veterinarian, holding the position for three years. Meanwhile, his artistic pursuits found him directing plays at a nearby cultural centre. After his veterinarian contract finished, Pars decided to pursue cinematographic studies in Moscow. "That was a crazy idea because I hardly knew any Russian. So I went there and they gathered the applicants together and explained the entry regulations. One prerequisite was a high school diploma and you had to have graduated during the Soviet era. Since I had already been a fourth year undergraduate university student at a Soviet university, this prerequisite seemed particularly stupid, but no, I was

told that I had to complete high school again! I had to graduate from a Soviet high school." Instead, Pars returned to Estonia and immediately went to Tallinnfilm Studio to see what jobs might be available.

Heino Pars, *Little Peter's Dream*, 1958.

Blessing Pars, as she did with many future Estonian animators, was Lady Luck, Fate, Destiny, whatever you wanna call her. The director of Tallinnfilm just happened to be around that fateful Thursday morning when Pars came to seek employment and told him that they were looking for a camera assistant. "If I could get my paperwork straightened out by Monday, I could have the job. I had to get myself registered in Tallinn because at that time I lived in Järva-Jaani. It was a crazy idea but I was lucky. City bureaucrats were reluctant to register people in Tallinn. I had a paper from Moscow, though, that stated that there is a prerequisite that must be completed before I can be admitted to the high school entrance examinations. Then I said that the prerequisite is that I have to gain practical experience at Tallinnfilm Studio. Naturally then, everything was in order, and I got the necessary papers."

But of course, it wasn't quite so easy. To be registered in Tallinn you had to have an apartment, which Pars did not. "I went from house to house in the suburbs with no luck. I happened by chance to have traded my apartment to a family whose daughter lived in Tallinn. She reached an agreement with her mother-in-law to register me at their address. That is how I found work at Tallinnfilm."

Pars was not assigned to the animation unit, instead engaged as a helper (as opposed to an assistant, which required more qualifications) to documentary film cameraman Vladimir Parvel. "I completed my training with Parvel and then I went from one cameraman to another for two years, during which time I travelled around Estonia. This was interesting for me of course. I got an overview of that life and got an introduction to very many lines of work. That was not bad." Pars was disappointed, though. He had hoped to find a stimulating artistic environment at Tallinnfilm but instead discovered "a rather meagre studio with directors from Moscow who were like leftovers."

During production gaps, Pars was often assigned to the new animation department. "Elbert Tuganov was there and they did film titles and credits and other animated shots. Tuganov started doing more artistic work as the inlay photography cameraman and they needed someone to film the credits. So I took over and there got more familiar with techniques of animation." When Tuganov was given the chance to make an animated film, he

needed a film crew. "I happened to be hanging about, he asked me to join him and that is how it all started.

Pars' promotion to directing made perfect sense. "I was used to that work," says Pars, "and I had seen how things were done. All you needed was the script and you had to know what to do with the script. I worked with [Estonian writer] Eno Raud and together we managed."

Pars was always approaching Tuganov with ideas for films and in 1961 he was finally given his first opportunity to direct. Initially, he made a test episode, and then came his first solo film, *Vaike motoroller* (Little Motor Scooter) in 1962.

After directing *Little Motor Scooter*, Pars and his team (including art director, Georg Stsukin and co-writer, Kalju Kurepold) created the first Estonian animation series, featuring the recurring character, Kõps the cameraman. In each film (there were four in the series), Kõps takes viewers on expeditions to various "exotic" locales like the Mushroom Land, Berry Forest, and Uninhabited Island.

In a sense, Kõps was based on Pars. "I had a strong connection to nature. My father had a large garden and I remember that springtime was the most beautiful when the apple trees were in bloom. Our trees were 30 years old then and when their branches touched each other, it was like a large roof of flowers. Back then I'd climb an apple tree and sit up there for hours."

But the *Kõps* series was more than a nostalgic return to youth, as each film also served an educational purpose. The characters didn't just walk around admiring the pretty flowers, they would also ask a local scientist, for example, questions about what they were encountering. "Our idea was that the viewer should learn something and that everything is interesting if you know something about that particular thing. That is why they turned out to have a kind of tendency toward popular science." Pars and his team spent a great deal of time researching their topics. For the fourth film *Operaator Kõps kiviriigis* (Kõps in the World of Rocks, 1968), Pars and his crew went to the Leningrad Museum of Natural Science and then visited a gold mine in Siberia. "We went down into the shafts but nothing much came of that. We had to strip down to our underwear when we came out, of course, to make sure we did not steal anything. We were very well received by the museum in Leningrad. The museum director was very friendly toward Estonia and the staff even brought things out of storage to show us wthat they normally would not have. I remember they brought out a beryl [a gemstone] that supposedly cost I don't

know how many million. They took it out of the safe. I was afraid even to hold it in my hands. That was very interesting indeed."

Children loved the series. "I remember meeting children on some occasions and seeing their reactions. When they saw on screen how a flower bud opens up and blooms or how a berry turns red, I could feel right away how the kids in the cinema were enthralled by the experience."

Like Tuganov, Pars made films with a child audience in mind. "It was not specifically required by Moscow [until the early 1970s]. I simply liked dealing with children. I had children of my own and I was in touch with children, so it suited me in that sense."

What is most interesting about the *Kõps* films, and especially the last one, is Pars' ability, which anticipated future Estonian animators like Janno Põldma, Heiki Ernits and Avo Paistik, to combine the pedagogical, poetic and philosophical. Although for children, the films are poetic, almost experimental, in their celebration of the beauty and mystery of the natural world. In *Kõps*, and especially in Pars' later films, *Elujõgi* (River of Life, 1986) and *Laulud Kevadele* (*Song of Spring*, 1975), there is even an element of pre-Socratic philosophy at play. Pars often expresses a sense of wonder not at man's conscience or intellect but at the basic material nature of the world, a wide-eyed fascination with the rhythm and form of the natural landscape.

The production schedule at Nukufilm was set up so that when one director finished a film, another was immediately ready to start the next. "When Pars started making films," says Tuganov, "we each had people we tended to work with and there were also some people we shared. There were two art directors and we each had one. Georgi Tsukin worked with Pars and I worked with a succession of different art directors. We had to have two cameramen because the production periods overlapped. Then we reorganized things so that each had his own crew but we still traded people back and forth. The staff of each crew was not rigidly defined."

The late Georgi Tsukin joined Nukufilm in 1962, having come from the Russian drama theatre. "He was a very talented, multifaceted man, and a very good chemist," says Tuganov. Tsukin's first solo job as art director (he had apprenticed on *Little Motor Scooter* and *Just Nii* (Just So), 1963) was on *Talent*. "This is when I noticed what a terrific guy he was," says Tuganov. "He asked what character one or another puppet should have. I answered that, for instance, one puppet is a spinster and a music teacher and she could be a little bit funny. That was all he needed to know. He hit the nail right on the head and made excellent puppets."

Previous page:

Top:
Heino Pars, *Old Mother Kunks*, 1977.

Bottom:
Heino Pars, *Old Mother Kunks and Captain Trumm*, 1978.

Pars, who worked with Tsukin until 1979, also strongly admired the Ukrainian. "He was an interesting man, very well informed regarding research in natural sciences. He had expert knowledge of mushrooms and drew illustrations for books about mushrooms. He was a very valuable man and he came up with many ideas that were valuable in our work." Pars used other art directors on occasion, but felt most comfortable with Tsukin. "He was absolutely irreplaceable in making nature films. He knew so much about plants. When we filmed nature, it was not so easy to work in those conditions. The puppet had to be fixed on a base and that has to be placed in a live natural setting. Wooden surfaces had to be covered with moss and bran. If we didn't thoroughly think things through, the picture would have been very chaotic and the result very ragged. We managed very well in this kind of work."

Aarne Ahi, who continues to work at Nukufilm today, started as an animator in 1967. "I remember my first impression quite well because I was sent to Nukufilm as a punishment. It was a weird impression. The studio was outside of Tallinn beside some bushes. There was a long building. It was dark. There were some lamps burning, huge tables and some person bending over the tables doing something and shooting, then bending and shooting again. It was clear to me that these people were mad."

Within a week or so Ahi found himself animating with these lunatics. "There was a conflict between Tuganov and another animator so he approached me in an imperative mood, put some film in the camera and let me animate. It was a sand beach with some monkeys on it. I worked about three or four metres in two days. Afterwards, when I saw it, I was fascinated."

Ahi enjoyed working with both Tuganov and Pars. "Stanislavsky noted two types of director: a dictator and democrat. Tuganov was the dictator and Pars was a democrat. It was exciting to work with both. Both of them were interesting. Tuganov prepares everything step by step and minute by minute and this can be quite interesting and with Pars it was the opposite. He just said 'say something tender' and we had to do it."

After Pars began directing, a new cameraman had to be found. A variety of people tried their hand at the camera: Kalju Kurepold and Ants Looman (who are discussed in the next chapter), and even Georgi Tsukin, (who shot *An Almost Unbelievable Story*). But it was Arvo Nuut who would shoot a majority of Nukufilm productions from 1961 until the late 1970s.

Nuut was born in Tallinn in 1941. "The first thing that influenced me was photography. As a young boy, I was fascinated by photography. At the age of 17, I worked for half a year at a film

Animator Aarne Ahi,
Balls (director
H. Pars), 1973

warehouse before going to Tallinnfilm." Before that, Nuut went to Tartu University to become a veterinarian but quit before completing his studies. He came to Tallinn in 1960 and through some contacts got a job as ... you guessed it ... a camera assistant at Tallinnfilm. Nuut's stay was brief. He was drafted into the Russian army. His only way out was to enrol in a post-secondary school, so he returned to Tartu and studied agriculture. His stay, again, was brief. The people at Tallinnfilm wanted him back.

Nuut's first film was *Ott in Space*, working as Pars' assistant. "He was my teacher," says Nuut. "Pars started to teach me right away because he was interested in filmmaking and he wanted a new cameraman." Nuut worked as an assistant on only two films before becoming a cameraman on Tuganov's *Lapsed ja Puu* (Children and Tree, 1965). "There were about 15 people employed when I started and the environment was really exciting and very creative. I can't imagine a better place for a young man to start. I was in the right place, right time."

Nuut worked frequently with both Tuganov and Pars and provides an interesting overview into their very different personalities and approaches. "Tuganov was German-educated and was pedantic with himself and toward other people. Pars was a more creative type. He was more down to earth and later on developed his own sort of philosophy and liked nature and things."

Nutt continues, "Tuganov followed a storyboard very strictly. In the morning he would prepare everything in detail and show it to the group. You could make minor changes but rarely big ones and when everything was clear, he said, 'see you in a week, I'm going to a festival now,' and he left the group to do what they had to do."

And of Pars, "His method was to animate the people first. He'd get them together, discuss everything in the smallest detail and the main thing was to elevate the people to some mental state. A large amount of time was spent creating this atmosphere. He himself was vibrating, smoking and talking to everyone so, when the film started, everyone was feeling this energy. Pars was open to changes. He had an ability to see in the air when something needed changes."

Undoubtedly, the different work styles of the two men and quiet competition between them was good for the studio. They continually challenged each other and, more importantly, themselves. But the question remains, why were there only two directors from 1961 till around 1975? There were many years when both Pars and Tuganov were making two films each per year. Just making one film per year would be a challenge for most filmmakers.

Arvo Nuut.   Certainly the films, for the most part, turned out OK, aided by a very loyal, professional and competent crew. So why were others not invited to make films?

"I was accused of working on my own for six years and not choosing anybody to join me," notes Tuganov. "Fair enough, I did not bring anybody new aboard, but I did not prevent anybody from joining the studio either. When Pars started making films, I did not do anything to obstruct his work. I got to make new films and I hung on to those jobs and gladly did the work. When Pars started out, then two of us did the work."

According to Pars, there simply weren't any people capable of directing – a strange comment given that neither Tuganov nor Pars had any directorial experience when they started. So just how would they know if there were no capable directors unless they tried them out? Interestingly, Pars does briefly mention that there was a "Russian woman who was truly offended that she did not get to be a director." And why did she not?

But what Tuganov and Pars fail to note is how the film community was quite a closed and privileged group. As we shall see in later chapters, most of the animators past and present knew someone who worked at the studio. So it's quite easy for Tuganov to say that he never stood in anyone's way and leave it at that. But from all accounts, Tuganov neither went out of his way to pass on his knowledge nor encouraged the training of new directors. So, by virtue of doing nothing, Tuganov, consciously or unconsciously, discouraged the development of new directors and closed the door to any potential newcomer. Was it perhaps a fear of competition? Tuganov was 'the man'. He called the shots and attended the international festivals. Perhaps he feared being supplanted in this distinguished position. Of course it's all speculative, as I doubt there was any submerged spite behind the scenes.

While Pars spent the 1960s focussed primarily on the *Kõps* series, Tuganov began alternating work on children's films with more adult themed satires and also began experimenting with cutout animation. Such films as *Park*, *Just Nii* (*Just So, 1963*), *Park* (1966), *Jonn* (Stubborness, 1966), *Hammastratas* (Cogwheel, 1968) and *Jalakaijad* (Pedestrians, 1971) gently mocked modern Soviet bureaucracy.

Pedestrians, a light critique of car culture based on a passage in the acclaimed Russian novel, *The Golden Calf,* by Ilya Ilf and Yevgeni Petrov, views the history of the world through the eyes of pedestrians.

Park is perhaps the most interesting and quietly subversive of Tuganov's 1960s films. People have walked through a local park

Elbert Tuganov,
Pedestrians, 1971.

for years and created a well-trod path. One day, bureaucrats (represented only by talking cut-out heads) decide to redesign the park with a newly paved path. They have a big Grand Opening for the park but everyone still follows the old, unpaved path. The baffled bureaucrats then erect signs and barbed wire. When this fails to change people's habits, they pave a new path with lots of curves and turns, but still the people follow the old path.

Park uses a cut-out style that is reminiscent of the world of Polish animator Jan Lenica or even the films of the National Film Board of Canada. (In fact, a number of Tuganov and Pars' films could easily have been products of Canada's state animation studio, an interesting parallel given their ideological differences.) While one can certainly read the film as a critique of those who refuse change, it seems as though Tuganov is suggesting that no amount of new rules and regulations will ever change the true nature of the people – in this case, the Estonian people.

Even some of Tuganov's child-oriented work of the time began to take on a more moral or satirical quality, in the vein of Czech animator Jiri Trnka. *Avipoeg Fips* (Fips The Monkey, 1968) is a Curious George-tinged story about a monkey whose curiosity leads him to be captured and brought to the city where he is sold to various merchants before finally escaping and returning home. *Hiirejaht* (Mousehunt, 1965) is a hilarious B-movie-inspired piece (complete with sombrero-topped mice twisting away to a sped-up Arvo Pärt rock-and-roll score) that borrows from spaghetti westerns and American teen movies to tell a Wild West tale about a group of bandit mice and their fat-cat enemies. *Aatomik* (Atomic Boy, 1970) and *Aatomik ja jommid* (Atomic Boy and the Warlord, 1970) were based on a famous Estonian children's book by Vladimir Beekman. Both films, in Cold War fashion, deal with the pros and cons of Atomic energy. In the first film, a scientist develops atomic energy (represented by a little atom character) only to lose control of it. The rest of the film then follows the scientist as he tries to capture the little atom. The message is simple: atomic energy equals power. In the sequel, a warlord steals the atom from the scientist so that he can use the atomic energy to gain military power. There are of course references here and there to the USA (the enemy of the time). In the end, the scientist creates a robot dog who rescues the atom boy, enabling him to destroy the military base. While the story might now inspire the anti-nuke among us, it's the innovative, almost experimental Arvo Pärt soundtrack (more a series of sounds than an actual composition) that stands out, along with the ingenious design and use of colour.

Elbert Tuganov,
Bloody John, 1974.

The most successful of Tuganov's parodies is *Verine John* (Bloody John, 1974). Based on a fairy tale by Juhan Peegel, the film is essentially a pirate spoof about a band of pirates who travel around robbing, killing and causing general havoc under the charge of their captain, Bloody John. The twist of the story comes from the human element, likely taken from the original story, that Tuganov grafts onto John. He is not the amoral cardboard cut-out stereo-type of most adventure stories. Yes, John is a fat, hard-drinking ladies' man, but he has a conscience when it comes to love. The crux of the tale involves the kidnapping of a beautiful rich gal, who becomes John's lover. Over time, the woman becomes comfortable with pirate life and grows increasingly greedy. In the end, she betrays John, shoots him, stirs up a mutiny and drives John so crazy that he flees to the countryside. There he meets a farmwoman; they marry, have kids, and John toils the soil.

Anticipating later puppet designs, Tuganov had puppets made out of cloth and a variety of found objects (rope, string, burlap), giving *Bloody John* an almost dirty, loose feel that perfectly suited the story and its lecherous, greedy characters. With its darkly comic and almost casual depiction of murder, greed and lust, *Bloody John* is among the most, for lack of a better word, risqué (if you find puppets made of rope to your liking!) films Tuganov made.

Before we catch up with Heino Pars, let's digress for a moment to hear Sylvia Kiik's amusing tale of the film Tuganov attempted to make after *Bloody John*:

> We tried to receive approval for the script of the puppet film *Tooth Marks on the Apple*, which Tuganov had planned as a parody. He wrote the script with feature film director J. Müür, basing it on a popular literary parody by Estonian writer J. Peegel. We sent the script ahead and flew to Moscow on the first plane on Monday morning. At the beginning of the workday we were met by the chief editor. His decision was negative – I will not support this scenario! We sat until the end of the day at the office of the chief editor at Goskino. We were asked in neither on this day nor the next. We travelled back to Tallinn, but on Thursday morn-ing we were back in Goskino. After lunch the secretary announced that the chief editor was at a plenum, lasting until Friday evening. A week had passed and we had no idea if the script would be rejected or if we could agree on making modifications. Early the following Monday morning we went to Goskino again. We waited until evening. At the end of the day the high superior found the time to tell us that the parody film had lost its relevance, that Goskino is not

Elbert Tuganov, *Atom Boy and the Warlords*, 1974.

interested in such films. However, parody was part of our accepted slate for the year. Because the head of the studio had a duty assignment in Moscow I had asked him to raise the issue of the rejected script again. Unfortunately, no positive result came of it, nor was he given a sensible reason as to why the script was unacceptable. It was difficult to believe that a genre had been banned but so was the case. The good intention of the director was drowned in the muddy flows of Goskino. Parody films were now gone from our yearly plan, yet there were 50 people in the crew who wanted to get paid. Thanks to Tuganov's experience we quickly managed to find material to replace it and avoid a longer stoppage of work.

What makes Tuganov's satires and parodies so interesting is that they fuse Estonian identity (through the characters and the many contributions of Estonian writers, musicians and artists) with aspects of Western culture. It is easy to see why children and viewers in the Soviet Union loved Estonian animation. It gave them not only a peek inside another culture, but also at another world. As Heino Pars noted in an interview, "they [Russians] regarded us rather well and they loved coming here for visits very much because being here was a little bit like being in the West."

"Our films were different from Moscow films," says Tuganov. "Each frame of a Moscow cartoon or puppet animation was filled. There was not even one square centimetre of clean surface. We here in Estonia had clear surfaces. We had breathing space and our colour tones were beautiful and somehow different." And in fact, the bright colour tones of which Tuganov speaks had roots in Pop Art and the lush, bright tones that we associate with 1950s American design and architecture. Whatever might be said about Tuganov's personality as a director, no one can quarrel with his open-mindedness as an artist. He exposed himself to a great deal of animation, film and art and obviously knew, through his travels especially, what trends were occurring in modern art at the time. "There was no information blockade," says Tuganov. "We saw the newer Disney films and so on. I attended the Ottawa festival [Canada] and other festivals many times, so I was not isolated."

Tuganov also came under the spell of Czech and British animation. "The Czechoslovakian school was an example for me. I looked up to two or three directors of feature films. Great Britain produced some very good puppet films. What they were like and how they were made was simply fantastic. It was terrific how they used different heads and how they moved one way and another. Simply, their technique and equipment were very good."

But the first man to capture Tuganov's attention was Alexander Ptushko, who made the puppet animation film, *The New Gulliver* (1935). "It used a human puppet and small clay puppets. I liked it very much. The Czechs saw it too, were enraptured, and started making puppet films. That this one man made one film in the Soviet Union, one small episode, and he could not be bothered to work in animation anymore ..."

While Tuganov has been deemed a dictator of sorts as a director, it's clear that he knew very well what he wanted to achieve in his films. "I personally had an agenda. Puppet films in general are somewhat clumsy because they are made with puppets whose motion is not always so clean and smooth. I required the puppet animators on my films to move the puppets one frame at a time. They could not be bothered, moving them two frames at a time, and that led to a conflict. They tried to fool me but I caught them right away."

Meanwhile, Pars made one of his strongest works and easily the most adult tale Nukufilm had produced: *Nael* (Nail 1972). Over a decade before John Lassiter (of the American computer studio, Pixar) went to all that digital effort to humanize lamps, unicycles, and snow globes, Pars, without computers, achieved the same effect using nails as his protagonists. *Nail* consists of four short comical stories dealing with such decidedly saucy topics as seduction, betrayal, drunkenness, and the ever-comical death.

Pars got the idea for *Nail* from his personal experience of woodworking. "I loved woodworking and carpentry and have built several cottages for myself. While hammering nails, some would be bent crooked. Then I'd admire such a nail and thought how expressive it was. It started to fascinate me and I thought I could make something out of this. I had to think up little banal story lines because the viewer had to understand it easily."

Pars ran into some problems because of the satirical nature of the film. Moscow was paranoid (rightfully so!) about every work of satire, fearing that it contained criticism directed at them (remember ... this was a few years before Tuganov's parody problem with Moscow). "I had to go to Moscow three times to voice proposals and explain the script. Then they wanted me to make more storylines that would fit onto a standard reel so that they could then pick and choose."

But the most imposing challenges facing Pars were technical. "It was a very difficult film to make even though it seems to be very simple. We had to find a material that could be easily bent. We tried using aluminium but it was no good because when you bend it back, it is no longer as clean a line as before. Someone even said

Heino Pars, *Nail*, 1972. that a mixture of gold and silver was best suited for this job. But we were not rich enough for this option of course. Finally we made the nails out of rubber and that is how we managed."

The next challenge was keeping the nails upright. As the nails were hanging from wires and shot in close-up, it was difficult to get them to stay fixed. Pars had to turn to the tools of illusion: mirrors. "We had to use mirrors 50 per cent of the time. We had flat surfaces and we reflected the nail so as to look like it was standing up. Then we also had to give the nail a shadow to make it look like it really was standing up. This was a very complicated assignment for Arvo Nuut (the film's cinematographer), but we succeeded together."

It's actually quite surprising that Pars did not have more problems with Moscow and censors. "I had a very bad past as far as they were concerned. My mother had been deported, so I had to lie whenever I filled out application forms. I was astounded that the KGB didn't bring it up." After independence, Pars had a chance to see his file in the KGB archives and it turned out that they were very familiar with him. "I don't know if I was just not caught or what. Even the fact that I was granted foreign visas was a miracle."

Like Tuganov, Pars had more problems with studio administrators than with Moscow. "Nonsense came up from time to time regarding *Nail*, for example, or small things like not using the word 'cosmos' in a film, because some cosmonauts had died," notes Pars, "but we managed." Ironically, these pedantic censorship problems are very similar to those in contemporary North American society.

Throughout the 1970s, Pars continued to fuse his love of nature with animation and the best results were the aforementioned *River of Life* and *Song to the Spring*.

Song to The Spring combines puppet animation with live-action backgrounds as an old man awakes with the day and conducts the forest birds, flowers, sun and grass to rise and sing. The mixture of puppet animation and live action is awkward at times. The puppet character does not add any special dimension to the film that could not have been achieved by a live actor. In fact, the film is essentially a live-action film. Nonetheless, Pars manages to express his love of nature enthusiastically yet gently, without crossing into the realm of cheesy new-age serenity. Nothing feels forced or deliberate; *Song to the Spring* emerges simply as a document of the new day and season, a celebration of re-awakening and the on-going process of being.

"It was originally planned entirely differently," notes Pars, "We tried shooting in the forest without much success. Trying to film

nightingales was the worst. This was solved during a trip to Minsk. There was a young engineer who loved catching birds. He kept them in cages. When he'd start shaving, his golden oriole would start to sing. I don't know why. He also had nightingales and other birds. We were able to film close-ups of them by holding them in our hands."

After working with insects on the *Kõps* films, Pars was quite excited by the challenge of working with birds. "Birds are particularly alert actors. They are not as easy to handle as insects, for example, which you can make sluggish by keeping them in the refrigerator. Such methods are out of the question for birds!"

River of Life is a fitting end to Pars' career (he did make two more films after that, but neither is particularly interesting). As the title suggests, the constant motion of the river symbolizes life. While there is a thread linking the film's images, ending with the birth of a child, the film is at times more akin to non-narrative experimental film. Pars seems mainly intent on capturing the fluidity, conflict and random beauty of the always-flowing river. Pars possesses a great eye for detail. He doesn't just blandly depict the water as a whole but shows us its individual drops in all their fragility and personality, and further takes us underwater to show us an assortment of forms, shapes and creatures. The river, like life, is marked by ebb and flow … this, now that.

During the latter half of the 1970s, coincidently, a time when new directors started to appear at Nukufilm, Tuganov's body of work became increasingly varied. He continued to make interesting (and not so interesting) films for children, along with a handful of technically audacious films including the astonishing time-lapse film *Inspiratsioon* (Inspiration, 1975) a document of the famous Estonian song festival, and two stereoscopic (i.e. 3D) puppet animation films, *Suvenir* (Souvenir, 1977) and *Õunkimmel* (The Dappled Colt, 1981).

Inspiration is perhaps Tuganov's finest achievement, at least conceptually. The film is a pixillated (or time-lapse) document of the preparations for, and performance of, the famous Estonian Song Festival. We witness the day's swift rise, then people dressing and assembling for the festival, and towards the film's end, a massive gathering of Estonians singing. The film is seemingly unremarkable in that it's just a gathering of people; a conventional chronology of a day in the life. But when one considers that this was Soviet-occupied Estonia during the repressive days of USSR President Leonid Brezhnev, the film is a monumental patriotic achievement. It stands as a subtle, yet ultimately overwhelming,

Elbert Tuganov
Inspiration, 1975.
celebration of Estonian culture in firm defiance of Soviet occupation.

Surprisingly, Tuganov faced no obstacles in making the film and even managed to capture some awkward footage of Moscow leaders. "Our song festival was known in the Soviet Union and it was part of the friendship between peoples. Be that as it may, they did not dare ban it, nor could they. There were some glorious moments, like when the people stand up during that one song, then the crowd gathered on that mountain also stood and that wave continued on to the front rows, until all the visitors and members of the party Central Committee from Moscow also had to stand. And then Mikojan asked our first secretary what it was, was it our anthem? He had to talk his way out of it and explain that it was not our anthem but a very important song and the theme of our song festival. In that sense, there was nothing suspicious as far as Moscow was concerned." Tuganov also escaped Moscow's detection by combining the documentary and animation approaches. By presenting his idea for *Inspiration* simply as a technical experiment, he was free to do as he pleased.

Inspiration was also deeply personal for Tuganov. "I saw the Estonian song festival of 1947. I was not in the country for the earlier festivals. The song festival was a moving experience for me every time and so I wanted to make that film." Anyone who wonders why the path to Estonian independence was called "The Singing Revolution" need only watch *Inspiration* to understand.

Tuganov was inspired to make a 3D animation film by a newsreel director named Peep Puks. Puks had become fascinated with 3D film technology after seeing the work of some Moscow filmmakers. So Puks and Tuganov visited Moscow to see various live-action 3D films. "The Russian technology was different from the American system," says Tuganov, "The Americans simultaneously projected film from three different projectors onto the same screen to create the effect. In the Russian system, the camera squashed the picture together into one frame. The lens of the projector decompressed the picture into 3D format and only one projector was needed. The negative was the same, only the frame was slightly larger." Upon returning from Moscow, Tuganov decided to make the first 3D puppet film in the USSR and encountered no objections from Moscow nor Tallinnfilm.

The creative process for *Souvenir* was the same as for any other puppet film, except that the animators had to allow for the specific parameters of 3D technology. "The camera had two parallel lenses," says Tuganov, "and so its field of vision was wider. The sets had to be larger to account for this. The technology did not dictate the size of the puppets, though. The puppets could be any size we wanted them to be. It was interesting work and it turned out well."

Elbert Tuganov, *Souvenir*, 1977.

The 3D process was so interesting to Tuganov that he made another stereoscopic film, *Dappled Colt,* which would turn out (although he didn't know it at the time) to be his final film. Tuganov turned 60 (the official retirement age for men in the Soviet Union) in 1982, retired from Nukufilm, and headed for what was supposed to be a holiday in Spain.

Tuganov notes in his autobiography that he was unhappy and fed up with life in the Soviet Union. He was tired of the way things were run, he was tired of the restrictions, and most of all he was tired of Leonid Brezhnev, who seemingly refused to retire despite being a mental and physical mess. (Word has it that despite being a drooling old fart, Brezhnev was kept around by the Politburo boys as a propped-up puppet so that they could do what they wanted). Tuganov had decided that when he reached Spain he would defect. During the trip, mostly accompanied by Moscow filmmakers, Tuganov kept looking for the right moment to make his escape. That opportunity hadn't presented itself by the time Tuganov was to fly back to Moscow from Madrid. "We were already at the airport," says Tuganov, "and my bags had been checked in. We were several hours early because our group leader got the departure time mixed up. While everyone else slept, I paced back and forth, moving farther and farther with each pass. Finally, I walked out of the airport, hailed a taxi and headed for the police station." Unfortunately, the police station was closed.

While he waited for the police station to open, Tuganov wandered about, trying to be as inconspicuous as possible. Finally, at 9am, the police station opened. "I made the great leap of faith when the police station opened but was informed that Spain did not offer political asylum, so I was handed over to the International Red Cross." The Red Cross housed Tuganov in a variety of hotels for a week before he was finally taken to a small boarding house just outside of Madrid run by nuns. During this stay Tuganov was asked where he wanted to apply for asylum. Because he had lived there as a youth, Tuganov chose West Germany. The Germans, however, didn't want him; they refused his application. Meanwhile, Brezhnev bit the dust.

Tuganov was at a loss: he hadn't expected West Germany to refuse him entry or that the man he loathed would be no more. So on 1 December 1982, Tuganov lost his desire to flee and turned himself in to the Soviet Embassy in Madrid. On 7 December, Tuganov was flown back to Moscow, where KGB agents asked him to write

Elbert Tuganov, *Souvenir*, 1977.

a detailed account of his stay in Spain. Tuganov was then put on a plane (with a KGB escort) and sent back to Tallinn. With his return came the condition that he continually check in with the local KGB. Furthermore, he had to explain his actions to his Tallinnfilm colleagues.

Tuganov eventually returned to Nukufilm as a consultant and proposed to make a stereoscopic film (it would have been his third) about Greek mythology. Goskino, however, was not interested in Tuganov's project. Tuganov later discovered that Tallinnfilm had in fact received a phone call from the Central Committee of the Estonian Communist Party telling them not to allow Tuganov to make any more films. (In the early 1990s, Tuganov proposed a project in celebration of the centenary of cinema which did eventually see the light of day – *1895* by Priit Pärn and Janno Põldma.)

What do Tuganov and Pars see when they look back at their 25 years of filmmaking? "I have not made a single film that I would dare refer to as a good film," says Pars, "But there are parts of every film about which I can say that this or that turned out well. I tend to cherish nature films more, but you cannot say that one of them is better or that another one of them is worse. There were very many mediocre films that I do not even want to see again."

"I am a product of that time," says Tuganov, "I gladly made films then and, at that time, I really wanted my films to differ from the stuff that came from Moscow. I wanted to make films my own way, not only visually but also technically. I often thought about how to technically achieve one thing or another, like in [*Inspiration*]. Nowadays I cannot relate to many things nor do I know how to relate to them. Things are so different now."

Rah-rah enthusiasm notwithstanding, we must keep in mind that Pars and Tuganov made a lot of films in a relatively short period of time. Tuganov made 36 films between 1957–1981, while Pars made 29 films between 1962–1990. That's extraordinarily prolific. And a hell of a lot of good films, films that remain virtually unseen today, let alone acknowledged by the international animation community.

While you can trace parallels between these early films and the more absurd or surreal musings of today's Estonian animators – continued use of Estonian musicians, artists and writers; black humour, almost child-like wonder at the natural world – these are less shared aesthetic or conceptual traits than basic characteristics of the Estonian character. Tuganov and Pars' influence was more technical or structural insofar as they set the table for future generations of animators at both Joonisfilm and Nukufilm. As self-taught animators, they (and that includes technicians Arvo Nuut, Kalju Kurepõld, Aarne Ahi ...) spent the 1960s finding their way, developing crews and production structures, tinkering here and there to find out what worked and what didn't. In the end, even though each contributor's position on the making of a film was very well defined and despite the question of a lack of directors, Tuganov, Pars and their crews certainly shared their knowledge with their younger colleagues, whose talents were shaped by past hard-won experiences. And, as we shall see, the one common trait that links Tuganov to the youngest, newest Estonian animators of today is the oral tradition. There is no formal animation education in Estonia and as such almost every animator has had to learn on the job, guided by the voices of the past.

That Tuganov and Pars achieved what they did within a very rigid and often absurd political system makes their contributions all the more impressive. Despite all the pressures and lack of formal training, Tuganov and Pars' legacy is an often ingenious, intelligent, funny, and yes, even charming body of work that is at once rooted in Estonian culture, yet strikingly cosmopolitan.

Chapter Four

The Missing Link

A s Rein Raamat established the first Estonian drawn animation studio, it was assumed that he was responsible for the first drawn animation films in 1972. But, as it turns out, his weren't the first, nor perhaps even the second. There were reports in 1930s' newspapers of a drawn animation film being produced in Tartu. It is unknown whether this film was ever finished, as no one claims to have seen it. And in the 1960s, a decade before Raamat's work, came that of Kalju Kurepõld and Ants Looman. So, giving credit where credit is due, I'd argue that the first creators of drawn animation films were Kurepõld and Looman, followed very closely by Ants Kivirähk.

Kurepõld and Looman made three drawn animations between 1964–68 for the Russian newsreel, *Fuse*. From about 1967 onward, they also made a variety of animated commercials for Reklamm film. And Kurepõld was also involved in the making of at least two drawn films (directed by Ants Kivirähk) for Eesti Telefilm in the early 1970s. Why Kurepõld's and Looman's work has been overlooked is likely related to the fact it was commercial and therefore considered of lesser artistic value. And as the films were made for a Moscow produced newsreel, perhaps Estonians do not wish to acknowledge these films for nationalistic reasons. Artistic value notwithstanding, these films and their creators earned a rightful place within Estonian animation history.

Ants Looman was born in Tallinn in 1930. His father worked in a shipyard and when World War II erupted, shipyard workers and their families were sent to Siberia. After the War, Looman's parents stayed in Russia, but he returned to Estonia with his younger brother. As their childhood home was now a bombed ruin, the boys lived with their aunt. Looman's younger brother had been deemed an enemy of the Soviet state, so Looman was prevented from attending university in Estonia. He opted for the

Kalju Kurepõld.

Moscow Film School (VGIK), where he studied film administration. Looman studied in Moscow from 1950–1955 and, as such, was in Moscow for Stalin's death. "The VGIK hostel was outside of Moscow and while Stalin's body was on display for mourners there were severe restrictions to travel, but we managed to enter by freight train to Moscow. Moscow was heavily guarded but we knew the centre of town inside and out and we climbed roofs, knew alleyways and managed to reach the place. It was quite depressing. People were sobbing; others were banging their heads. We were scared that someone would see that we were not sobbing."

When Looman returned to Tallinn in 1955, he inquired about prospects at Tallinnfilm but they didn't need administrators for feature films. They did, however, need administrators for their puppet animation films. "Someone who really wanted to leave Nukufilm told me about the job. Essentially all I did was chase down hammers and nails, so it wasn't very exciting. But I actually was the one who employed Kalju."

Kalju Kurepõld was born in Tallinn in 1937. He studied to become a veterinarian at Tartu University but as animal healing didn't really strike his interest his stay was brief. (It wasn't all a waste, though – he did meet his future wife during his studies.) After dropping out, he turned his attention to athletics and joined the national rowing team. During his spare time he started doodling and making caricatures. Meantime, Kurepõld was struck by the fact that many of his fellow athletes didn't think of a life beyond sports and neglected their education. He didn't want the future that that would entail.

Kurepõld's first caricatures were published in 1959 thanks to his colleague Edgar Valter. "He encouraged me to continue drawing cartoons," says Kurepõld, "and I'd bring him over tons of caricatures. He'd pick some out and take them over to Pikker magazine to have (them) published."

In 1960, Kurepõld learned that animation films were being made at Tallinnfilm. "I had no idea what animation films looked like but I dialled the number and was told that they needed cameraman's assistants." Kurepõld began at Tallinnfilm working in the titles department. Sometime in 1961, Heino Pars, who was between films and needed to make some money, was also working in the titles department. Pars invited Kurepõld to come over to the Nukufilm division and work as both camera assistant and animator on the next Tuganov film, *Murri and Me (1961)*. In typically Estonian fashion, Kurepõld gained experience by just being thrown into the fire. "Tuganov was the only one with any

Ants Looman,
*Kõps on an
Uninhabited Island*
(director, H. Pars),
1966.

experience," says Kurepõld, "and his style of teaching was simply to take it and do it." Kurepõld was instantly taken with the open environment at Nukufilm: "the atmosphere was very good. What counted was a good idea and it didn't matter who came up with the idea. Hierarchy was not a big concern then."

When Pars began to direct films at Nukufilm in 1962, Kurepõld was 'promoted' to cameraman. The first film he shot was *The Little Motor Scooter* (1962).

At the time, the puppet studio was located outside of Tallinn. Every day, everyone rode to the studio. "I didn't like going there every morning," says Kurepõld, "I had no time to deal with my caricatures." Around 1963, Kurepõld started to talk with Looman about doing something different. "I wanted to get rid of my camera job," says Kurepõld, "and Ants was tired of the administration job." Neither man was particularly interested in puppets. They preferred drawing, but as neither of them had any power or influence, there wasn't much they could do. When Pars made the first of his *Cameraman Kõps* films, both Looman and Kurepõld were working as cameramen (Looman as an understudy to Kurepõld). It was during this time that they found a solution to their problems.

Moscow produced a live action/animation newsreel called *Fuse*. *Fuse* was filled with criticism of Russian bureaucracy and its impact often led to the loss of jobs in the Kremlin. The first screenings of the newsreel apparently were held in the Kremlin. Kurepõld made a storyboard based on a satirical script by Looman. When no one in Estonia showed any interest in their story, Looman, using his Russian contacts, tried his luck in Moscow. The administrator of Fuse was Sergei Mikhalkov, father of the famous filmmaker, Nikita Mikhalkov. Furthermore, Sergei Mikhalkov authored all three versions (Stalinist, post-Stalinist, and current Russian Federation) of the famous Soviet national anthem. Looman knew Mikhalkov from his school days in Moscow. Mikhalkov liked Kurepõld's storyboard and gave the two men approval to make the film. The film would be produced at Tallinnfilm, with all the production money coming from Moscow.

After the approval meeting with Mikhalkov, Kurepõld and Looman went over to Soyultzmultfilm where they got some quick tips on making drawn animation films. Kurepõld recalls, "Those people in Soyultzmultfilm were very kind, they showed us how to do things and provided materials (cels, film negative etc. …).

Kurepõld and Looman's first *Fuse* project became *Pine Cones* (1965), a mild parody of Russian bureaucracy in which people are told to go and collect all the pine cones in a forest. Doing so ruins the forest. Then, instructed to rebuild the forest, they re-plant all the pine cones.

Making the film turned out to be far more complicated than getting the initial approval. *Pine Cones* was a somewhat underground production because of its lack of official studio affiliation. "We had a friend in the centre of town," says Kurepõld, "and he had a studio. We used five students from the Estonian State Art Institute to do the in-betweens and clean-up [some of these students are now well-known Estonian artists: sculptors Aime Kuhlbusch and Aili Avari, graphic artist Ago Kivi and architect Külli Ehrenbusch]. We used cameras wherever we could get access to them." Along with these obstacles came the winter weather of 1964, which (actually) proved to be beneficial.

The two men were still working at Nukufilm, riding the bus daily for the 10km journey to the studio. On one winter morning, however, the bus couldn't get through to the studio because of the accumulated snow. "So we took the girls and all our stuff," says Kurepõld, "and went to Nukufilm and worked there in peace for two weeks until the snow melted. We didn't even pick up the phone there." It took Looman, Kurepõld and their three student artists almost six months to finish the film. *Pine Cones* premiered in Moscow in April 1965 and then screened all over the Soviet Union before feature films (in theatres). "This was seven years before the great white father started making any films," says Kurepõld, referring to Rein Raamat.

After the *Pine Cones*, working conditions improved for Kurepõld and Looman. They were given premises by the Tallinn city government. Looman devised a special multi-camera for their work and they had their own personal unit. The Tallinnfilm folks were not thrilled with this situation, even though they were receiving compensatory money for the use of camera, lights and supplies. In their eyes, the enterprise was a lot of work for very little money. But Tallinnfilm backed off when Kurepõld and Looman threatened to complain to *Fuse*. "Tallinnfilm couldn't do anything about it," says Kurepõld, "because we were employees of Moscow." Kurepõld and Looman made two more films for *Fuse*: *Lightning Rod* (1966) and *Two Heads are Better Than One* (1968). Each about three or four minutes in length, both films were light satirical pieces. *Lightning Rod*, for example, was based on one of Kurepõld's cartoons (by this time he was a well known caricaturist) about gossipy old women. "Two people are in love, but can't get rid of the women spying on them. The couple flees to an island but the old women show up there, too." Looman wasn't as involved in the *Fuse* films after *Pine Cone*. He was still working at Nukufilm and his main role on *Fuse* productions became that of a supplier, (bringing film, paper or ink to the *Fuse* staff every time he went to Moscow with film).

By 1968, the *Fuse* work began to overwhelm Kurepõld. Like Looman, Kurepõld was still working at Nukufilm as well as doing commercial work for Eesti Reklammfilm (Estonian advertising film studio). "Actually, salaries were quite small in those days," says Looman, "so we took different jobs. The most profitable thing to do was to write screenplays and the best thing was that you got paid twice. First when it was ready and later when it was copyrighted. The copyright money was the money your wife didn't know about!" One screenplay fetched the equivalent of about a month's pay.

Before their affiliation with *Fuse* ended, Kurepõld and Looman made a very nice final gesture. "We still had a unit allocated to us," says Kurepõld, "so we tried to find a use for it. At that time the Tartu University library was in very poor condition so we sent a cameraman to film the library and submitted the footage to *Fuse*." The screening brought so much attention that money was found for a new library.

When Joonisfilm was established in 1971, they used all of the old *Fuse* equipment. Rein Raamat even asked Looman to be a cameraman, but he refused because "filming drawings was not so exciting." Besides, Looman had already felt harassed at Nukufilm so he wondered if Joonisfilm would be any different. Looman had plenty of job offers in documentary and newsreels. When he retired, he had made over seventy documentaries.

It seemed logical though that Kurepõld would join Joonisfilm given his experience making drawn films, but it wasn't to be. "I couldn't get along with Raamat. I can appreciate his work but not him as a person. There wasn't enough space for the both of us." Strangely, given their experience, none of the three student artists that made up Kurepõld's and Looman's old unit were hired by Joonisfilm either.

Kurepõld and Looman went to work with Eesti Telefilm (ETF). ETF was established in 1965 as a division of Estonian Television (which was founded in 1955). ETF was responsible for creating original productions for Estonian Television (ETV) including feature films, music films, documentaries, and a handful of animation films.

Looman did titles and all sorts of odd jobs at ETF while Kurepõld worked on two short animation films, *Huvilist filmikaamerat* (The Curious Cameraman, 1971) and *Selliste lugudega* (Those Stories,

1973). Both of these films were directed by Ants Kivirähk and designed by artist Jaak Palmse.

Kivirähk had been an actor in the drama and puppet theatres of Estonia and was one of the first directors at ETF. He directed a feature film (*To the Cold Land*), several documentaries and the above-mentioned animation films. These were the only two animation films he made. Later on, he directed a TV puppet show called *The Adventures of Muffin* (about a small donkey boy).

After graduating from the Estonian State Institute of Art in 1956, Jaak Palmse (1931–1980) found work as an artist at ETV in 1956. In 1965, Palmse was hired as the art director of ETV and later, ETF. He made animated opening sequences for eighteen TV shows including the popular *Telepoiss* (TV Boy). The *TV Boy* opening was made in 1962 using a cut-out technique. (In 2002, the *TV Boy* character was revived by ETV).

According to his widow, Palmse was very interested in animation (apparently he made a short animated film by himself called *Feast* in 1970) and started working in the field out of pure enthusiasm. He liked precise drawing and artwork, and designed decorative leather covers and bookbindings on the side. Palmse continued working in animation until 1976 when his new duties as chief artist of Estonian Commercial Film (a division of ETV) meant that he no longer had time to continue with animation.

"I was the character designer on these films," says Kurepõld of his contribution to Kivirähk's films. "Again, art students did the in-betweens and clean-up. Estonian television had a rostrum animation stand for filming credits and titles, which was put to use in cartoon animation."

The general lack of animation experience shows as neither film (both are aimed at children) is particularly inspiring. "The films were not so good," says Kurepõld, "They were too long and lacked the punch that an animation film should have. Palmse did not know how to animate figures and Kivirähk did not know anything about directing animation films. He had directed chronicle and newsreel films but didn't have a grasp of the specific nature of animation films, how they have to be more concentrated." Maybe the Estonian Television bosses also recognized the shortcomings of these films as they elected not to make any more.

Reklaam Film, the central television commercial studio of the Soviet Union, was founded in 1969. While it happened to be located in Tallinn, it was completely independent from Tallinnfilm. Kurepõld and Looman worked at Reklaam, producing animation commercials of a sort. The creation of Reklaam was a major reason why they stopped making shorts for *Fuse*. There was lots of work to be had, with surprising flexibility: "It was a good time," says Kurepõld, "because I mostly worked at home and had no set hours." Kurepõld worked on around 200 commercials for a wide variety of clients. "In those days," says Kurepõld, "all factories and producers had a certain amount of money for advertising. They had to spend it because it was part of the planned budget. So as not to get reprimanded, they had to be rid of this money. Print ads weren't an efficient way of wasting money, so clients became interested in film because it cost a lot more. We were happy, though, because there was a lot of work and it paid better than Tallinnfilm."

The Reklaam studio occupied two houses located in Tallinn's Town Hall Square, in what is now a Russian restaurant. Once in a while Nukufilm and Joonisfilm animators like Tuganov, Pars and Paistik worked on commercials. (No one has yet located these commercials.) "We felt some jealousy from the art side because everyone wanted to do it," says Kurepõld, "but overall we all maintained good relations." The biggest problem with commercial work was that every client had come up with his own 'brilliant' script and would insist that the film follow it. "Generally these scripts were quite stupid and we had to convince clients that this wasn't the way to go."

For the most part, promoting a product or topic was less important than the client spending his budget and the filmmaker making money. Standard commercials run anywhere from 30 seconds to one minute, but many of Reklaam's films lasted three minutes and one particular film about traffic clocked in at twenty minutes. Quite often, these films were made just to earn money. Notably, Kurepõld remembers a documentary about a St. Petersburg chicken farm: "We had to animate segments to show the stupid things that chickens do, but it was well paid."

Unfortunately (depending on your taste), many of these films were not shown to the public. Most of the films were simply returned to the commissioning clients, who only showed them to a select audience of their own clients and guests. The lack of public exposure partly explains why this aspect of Estonian animation production has been overlooked. Another explanation is the usual art-over-commerce bias of critics and historians. "It was an interesting period," adds Kurepõld, "because very few of the films were rejected. We could experiment quite a bit and try all sort of techniques." Reklaam remained open until about 1993, but both Kurepõld and Looman left the previous year.

Looman continued working as a cameraman on puppet films, directed a children's film called *Punane, kollane, roheline* (Red,

Yellow, Green, 1982), worked on feature films and, when there wasn't a film in production, worked in the animation department at Nukufilm doing titles and whatever else that was required. He did this until retirement in 1992. An unofficial retirement though, as he continued to make documentary films until the mid-1990s.

Kurepõld made two films in Kazhakstan ("using men off the street as a film crew"), published a few caricature books in the 1990s, and did some commercial work, including commissioned work for Japan. He continues to make animation films as a hobby in his home, where he has an old animation camera and stand set-up.

Clearly the contributions of these men (Kurepõld, Looman, Kivirähk and even Palmse) need to be recognized by both international and Estonian animation historians. Even a recent Estonian television series about animation failed to acknowledge their work. (The history of Estonian animation – as it stands- needs a re-write, with the careers of these men adding an entirely new chapter.)

But hey, does it really matter who was first? The more important issue here is that there appears to have been a lot of undocumented animation activity on television and advertising in Estonia. Estonian animation can no longer be defined as the sole terrain of Nukufilm and Joonisfilm.

For their part, Kurepõld and Looman are quite modest about their silent pioneer status: "To be honest," says Kurepõld, "we are not very much acknowledged but we haven't pushed it either."

Let this chapter serve as a long overdue push.

Chapter Five

The Preachers

Rein Raamat

Rein Raamat was born almost directly in the middle of Estonia in a town called Türi. His parents were artists and from quite early on Raamat was pretty set on becoming an artist too. As early as secondary school, his teachers were instilling in him an enthusiasm for art. His interest in film came about through photography, but the only option for studying film was in Moscow. To study in Moscow though, you needed permission from the appropriate authorities and an ability to speak some Russian. Unable to do so, Raamat was rejected and instead enrolled in the Tallinn Art Institute, where he spent six years working on painting and drawing, and learning art history. Life at the art institute was, according to Raamat, quite tense: "Our rector didn't speak a word of Estonian and one of the first things he did was to cover antique sculptures with fig leaves. Our teachers during Stalin's time were accused of nationalism and formalism. It was a horrible period because some of the teachers committed suicide or became invalid. The ringleaders were Russian students who attacked our celebrated artists and lecturers. This was the atmosphere within which I studied."

At graduation Tallinnfilm studio representatives and artists from Lenfilm saw Raamat's work and offered him a job at Tallinnfilm as an artist on feature films. Raamat worked as a background and set artist doing sketches on a dozen or so films, but he wasn't thrilled with feature filmmaking: "Most of the films were not very good and the process of making a film took almost a year. I feel these years were wasted."

Meanwhile, Elbert Tuganov had seen Raamat's work and invited Raamat to join his puppet film team in the same capacity as he had fulfilled at Tallinnfilm. Raamat's stay at Nukufilm was relatively short, leaving in 1960 after only three years. He was invited to work on a film by filmmaker Herbert Rappaport. Rappaport had trained in Hollywood and at UFA in Germany (he was an assistant to G.W. Pabst) and, as such, knew the ins-and-outs of the filmmaking process better than most. Rappaport became one of Raamat's most important teachers, giving him the opportunity to see all aspects of the filmmaking process. From Rappaport came the solid base from which to start making his own animation films.

Raamat spent the 1960s working on feature films and absorbing everything he could about the process. "We had the opportunity to see films that were not in the usual Hollywood style. I saw filmmakers analysing and trying to make some kind of sense out of the present day and what was going on in human relationships and in society. That was something that really interested me and it was then that I became fascinated with the idea of starting a drawing studio."

Founding Joonisfilm, a drawn animation division within Tallinnfilm, was no easy task under a planned economic system where activities were staked out five years in advance. "There was no budget to make animated cartoons but for some reason a little bit of money was found for this purpose. I managed to organize a competition to hire people and many people came to Tallinnfilm to apply for jobs." Out of the 300 or so applicants, only fourteen were selected to be animators.

Unlike Nukufilm productions, Raamat was eager to make artistic animation for an adult audience. In fact, he was able to do so largely because of Nukufilm. "During this time, 70 per cent of the films had to be targeted to children, so I was able to avoid them because Nukufilm was fulfilling this quota." Some of the early Joonisfilm animators were even disappointed that they were not making children's films.

As almost none of the Joonisfilm crew had any experience making cel animation films, including Raamat, animators from Moscow often visited the studio to help guide the young animators, deliver lectures and provide consultation. For his own training, Raamat went to Moscow to study with famed Russian animator, Fedor Khitruk. Khitruk took Raamat under his wing reluctantly and cautiously, however, as Raamat was a complete unknown. Khitruk provided invaluable support to Raamat, teaching him the fundamentals of script-writing, translating script onto film and building film into sequences. Raamat found himself free to express his own ideas despite the environment and censorship. According to Raamat, "Khitruk was the one that I would always discuss each project with. He would go through the story, the thematic line and plot line, so his role was that of a professional sounding board, someone to discuss my ideas with and maybe clarify some points. He gave professional advice on certain things. Certain scripts he

would say, 'just put that aside, it's not worth doing.' It was never of a political nature, it was always on a professional level."

Meantime, Tallinnfilm had no studio space for the new division, so for the first year or two, Joonisfilm was housed in a variety of strange and often uncomfortable venues. Initially the animators worked at the song festival grounds. Four people worked at one long table, but when one was erasing it shook the entire table and disrupted the others (they later sawed the tables into shorter ones).

Joonisfilm's second location was an army building, but when the army began recruiting, the animation unit had to move, finding a hostel in the music academy. Their stay again was short lived. "Someone reported us," says Raamat, "The minister of education came, slammed his fist on the table and said that we must leave within 2 weeks."

Finally, Joonisfilm animators moved to an unheated seaman's club where they made their first two animation films wearing coats and gloves during a cold November and December. "Pretty soon the director of Tallinnfilm approached me and said that we had been given space in Tallinnfilm," says Raamat, "This was the moment we felt accepted because we had also just completed our first two films *Veekjanda* (The Waterman, 1972) and *Vari Ja Tee* (A Shadow Away, 1972)."

To get a film made at that time, you first needed a script. It was shown to the studio's editor whose job it was to provide feedback and get the script to Moscow for approval. "It's what you absolutely needed in order to get the film approved for production," says Raamat, "You would have to have the storyline worked out in detail. You had to know exactly what you were going to do. You couldn't just go with an idea and say 'give me money.'"

While Raamat often served as his own editor, the studio's principal editor of animation films was Sylvia Kiik. Her role with Joonisfilm was the same as it had been with Nukufilm, but now she faced more pressures as more adult animations were being produced. With Nukufilm, at least initially, there had been no special control. Manuscripts were sent to Moscow for introductions, and approval usually required modifications in the form of omissions. But when the animation repertoire began to include adult films, the control became more and more stringent. "Animation films were declared to be for children in the entire Soviet Union," says Kiik, "A plan was set for us – two thirds of the yearly production had to be films for children. We only had permission for one third of the output to be films for adults. Together with Joonisfilm's directing staff, we were able to almost reverse that relation. To call the studio to order a very effective measure was taken: thematic planning was rejected. This caused a mess. Our operative plan had to be changed. A suitable theme for a children's film and a director to take on the project had to be found quickly. It had to be delivered to Moscow in time for the meeting of the acceptance board, who reviewed, proposed plans and determined the fate of the next year's production. Only after the acceptance of the plan did the studio have the right to present literary scripts for review."

Interestingly, Tallinnfilm was not a subsidised institution; they needed bank loans to fund their films. Goskino, after approving a screenplay, was the guarantor of the loan. If any changes were made to the planned film, the bank could demand its money back immediately. It was Kiik's job to ensure that this never happened.

Raamat's films were in stark contrast to the early puppet films, so it's easy to understand Moscow's unease. Deeply metaphoric and embedded in Estonian folklore, Raamat's films are notable for their meticulous drawings, philosophical themes, and lack of humour. Additionally, Raamat opened up the doors between animation and other arts by continually collaborating with Estonian writers (Paul-Eerik Rummo), musicians (Lepo Sumera) and especially artists (Aili Vint, Leonard Lapin, Jüri Arrak, Priit Pärn, Edward Viiralt).

Raamat's first two films, *The Waterman* and *Shadow Away*, are passable Zagreb film imitations. Zagreb animators had visited Tallinn in November 1970 to show their films and Raamat admits that he was heavily influenced by what he saw. It's in his subsequent films *Lend* (The Flight, 1973), *Varvalind* (Colourbird, 1974), *Kilplased* (The Gothamites, 1974) and *Rüblik* (A Romper, 1975), that we begin to see something more unique, although it must be said that much of the power of these films stems as much from the artists involved as it does from Raamat.

In *Flight*, scripted by Estonian poet Paul-Eerik Rummo and designed by artist Aili Vint, a bored man sits on the ground. He sees a dandelion float by, gets up and chases after it. Once he catches the flower, he is carried higher and higher. With *Flight*, we see the first example of Raamat's career-long interest in the spiritual and philosophical condition of humanity. "Life is always changing and going on and upwards towards higher levels," says Raamat, "This was an idea that fascinated me. Rummo and I talked about these subjects a lot and he agreed to write the script for the film and this idea of flight seemed to be the best way to express these thoughts."

Graphically, *Flight* is distinguished from the Zagreb influence, but its use of a melange of blue tones, 'flowery' graphic style, rock music score and heavy symbolism are clearly rooted in the hippie aesthetics of the time.

Leonard Lapin's Pop/Avant-garde tendencies, expressed through cold, smooth, minimal geometric renderings of city blocks, are evident throughout Raamat's next film, *Colourful Bird*. A black and white city becomes more vibrant as it acquires colours and shapes. The children, who were blasé and robotic at the film's beginning, become more energetic and enthusiastic as more colours appear. Overlooking the city is a bright coloured bird. But when one colour dominates the city, peace is threatened – signalled by the appearance of a nasty little black cat. In the end, the cat and the bird appear to fight. The bird absorbs all of the colours to become a gigantic multi-coloured bird. And … hey I ain't gonna explain the symbolism to you.

The pairing of the conservative Raamat with Lapin, the father of the Estonian avant-garde, is an odd one. Lapin, for his part, can't even remember the circumstances, but he figures that it was through his Russian avant-garde friends, such as animators Eduard Nazarov and Andrei Khrzhanovsky, that Raamat (who had a great eye for talent) got word of his work.

Although the film's power comes primarily from Lapin's images, he actually had very little to with *Flight*, "I made the images, gave them to Raamat and he made a film." One image did change however. Lapin had initially made the bird white, but the censors insisted that it be one colour. Of course, a white dove was, and remains, a strong Western symbol of peace.

Colourful Bird, with its hippie ideology and pop-art graphics, influenced, whether directly or indirectly, later animators like Priit Pärn and Avo Paistik. In fact, a scene in *Colourbird* featuring a group of young people hanging out and mindlessly performing the same mundane actions over and over is reminiscent of scenes from Priit Pärn's later *Hotel E* (1992), in which he uses a similar pop-art look and slow motion pace.

Raamat's next films, *The Gothamites* and *A Romper* are noteworthy in as much as they serve to introduce Priit Pärn. Here began the animation career of the graphic artist who would revolutionize Estonian animation and strongly influence animators the world over. But we'll get to Pärn later on in the story.

While *The Gothamites* was taken from a story by Estonian literary pioneer F.R. Kreutzwald, *A Romper* was Raamat's only attempt at a children's story. The story was devised as a simple moral tale: a boy ignores a 'keep off the grass' sign and is turned into a little pig. However, Priit Pärn and artist Karel Kurismaa added some gently subversive touches to transform the cautionary tale into a

critique of the anal absurdities of bureaucracies. "The first story had no irony in it," notes Pärn, "Our contribution was to add the absurd configuration of the road and to make the caretaker, who was supposed to be a positive type, visually repulsive. I think it succeeded." The touches were so subtle that it's unclear whether Raamat even noticed.

Raamat's first international success and the first film in which he really seems to have found his voice was *Kütt* (The Hunter, 1976), a parable about a man's relationship with nature, adapted from Hemingway's *The Old Man and The Sea*. "I liked the general idea expressed by Hemingway: the tragedy of this man who does this hard work and has everything taken away from him. But in the end, I changed the final idea and turned it into something about greed and how it brings doom to you." In Raamat's story, a hunter harpoons a whale and, after his rope snaps, is pulled into the sea by the strength of the whale. Just as the hunter is about to die, the whale spares him by returning him to safety on an iceberg.

The Hunter is intricately and professionally drawn and the transition between images is quite unique, adding another layer of tension to the film. Using a slow-motion, time-lapse approach, each image dissolves directly into the next. "The transitions had to do with traditional painting composition," says Raamat, "and it also gives the rhythm to the film." This slow-motion style also emphasizes the importance and detail of each image, which could stand independently as a work of art.

The film's realistic style led some to assume that Raamat had used a rotoscopic technique – a process that involves shooting live action footage and then tracing and painting over the footage–but in fact the style stemmed from Raamat's detailed pre-production research. Raamat and his team visited various Moscow museums and archives, researching whales and whale hunting. Many of the film's ideas developed out of this preparatory research work.

Nevertheless, for all its formal accomplishments, *The Hunter* is dated and one-dimensional, calling attention to the shortcomings of most folklore and myth by its lack of complexity and subtlety. Raamat, as he does in most of his films, compartmentalizes the intricate and contradictory layers of human nature into stereotypes and in doing so sucks the very soul out of his characters. The hunter, as told by Raamat, is just a heartless killer. We are given no insight into his motivation (maybe he has a family to feed) and as such are left with little more than a cardboard cut-out version of humanity.

Control over production became significantly tighter by 1979 when the Soviet Cinema Committee created a new system of monitoring animation production. Goskino was given more editorial powers: it now not only had to see the film script, but also the storyboards and treatments. For the first time there were attempts to actually control the design of a film. On paper, Goskino now controlled every aspect of the creative work. Of course, Kiik and company always managed to find ways around these limitations.

Raamat's most significant films (he did make the very poetic *A Field* in 1978, but it is little more than an extension of the ideas explored in *The Hunter,* although expressed through a farmer and his horse) are *Suur Tüll* (Big Tyll, 1980) and *Pörgu* (Hell, 1983). Both films draw exclusively on Estonian culture for their style and content. **[NB see Great Töll in Estonian version!]**

Big Tyll is based on an old Estonian legend which dates back to the medieval period and the former slave island of Saaremaa. Big Tyll is an Estonian folk hero who comes to the defense of his people and his country when called upon. The film is designed by the famous Estonian artist Jüri Arrak, and features a haunting score by Estonian composer Lepo Sumera.

What is most remarkable is that Raamat was even able to make such a fervently nationalistic film during an anti-national cultural period. Throughout Soviet occupation, Estonian dissent never completely fizzled out. Remarkably, one of the last Forest Brothers, members of the infamous guerrilla resistance, continued his fight until 1978, when he drowned himself rather than succumb to capture by KGB men. There were many cases of violent and especially non-violent dissenters throughout occupation, but the cases were mostly of isolated individuals or small underground groups. This is not to suggest that Estonians gave up. On the contrary, it appears that Estonians learned to protest and sabotage internally. In the early 1980s protests began to steadily grow – most notably following the riot in Tallinn by 3000 youths at the banning of a pop concert. This youth rebellion spread to other cities and led to the famous "Letter of Forty". The letter, written primarily by poet Jann Kaplinski, detailed Estonians' feelings towards the Russification of their culture and how it stimulated protest against the Soviets. The letter called for less repression and more debate. The letter was signed by a variety of Estonian cultural figures and was published in Estonian newspapers. Such actions of resistance led to new Soviet restrictions upon the expression of national culture in art. It was within this climate that Raamat made these two strongly nationalistic films.

"I wrote the script based on this folk tale," says Raamat, "It didn't raise suspicions because folk tales and fairy tales were seen as harmless." Raamat's biggest challenge came in finding the design for the film. The production team worked for months on designs and drawings but nothing met with Raamat's satisfaction. Eventually, Raamat decided to approach Estonian artist Jüri Arrak for help.

Rein Raamat,
Great Töll, 1980.

"Raamat called me and at first it was strange," says Arrak. "He wanted a battle between Germans and Estonians. I said, 'I don't agree; It's a mythology.' I felt that the enemy must not be so concrete. And, anyway, we've had many enemies: Sweden, Denmark, Russia etc.' Estonia is like a corridor; there is always someone coming through. It's bad when someone stays too long in that corridor." Arrak eventually agreed to design the film but insisted on complete artistic control. Within a few weeks, Arrak produced the drawings of the main characters and then taught the animators how to carry on in his style.

Before the film was finished, Raamat faced a few humorous, in hindsight, problems. It was essential that the enemy not be represented by the colour red as it would be associated with the Russians. "I made the enemy lilac but our film stock was so bad that it came out red," says Raamat. The poor quality of the film stock was a constant problem for cinematographer Janno Põldma, here working on his first film: "No matter how good you tried to make the film, in five or six years it would be all red. The goal was to get a quality picture for the first few years. We tried to use more contrast in the pictures. If the shooting was made in a normal level, the colours started fading, but if a high contrast was used, it was more likely to survive. The film stock didn't contain silver… that was being used in the space industry and who knows where else." When politically correct Raamat saw the newly red enemy, he freaked, "what to do, what to do, now it's happened … it's political." To fix the problem, he put a blue filter behind the film and subsequently changed all the colours.

At this point, Arrak wanted out of the project, but Raamat pleaded with him to stay. Then the duo faced a second problem: Tyll's eyes were blue, black and white, the colours of the Estonian flag. At the time it was forbidden to show the colours of one's flag. Arrak simply explained that, "hey, I have eyes of the same colour. They are ordinary Estonian eyes. Then it was okay."

Like *The Hunter*, *Big Tyll* is bold, expressive and tense. *Big Tyll* is interesting for the way Raamat merges the personal with the epic. While the Tyll character possesses superhero-like characteristics, he is as domestic and fragile as those he protects. He helps his fellow locals and saves fishermen from drowning. He doesn't want to go to war nor does he want to kill. But, at the same time, he

Rein Raamat,
A Hunter, 1976.

cannot sit back and watch his people get slaughtered. One of the film's most moving and human images occurs when Tyll returns home to find his home destroyed and his wife slain. He is fraught with despair and sorrow. The murder leads to Tyll's final monstrous assault on the opposing soldiers and his subsequent death. A fiery, forebodingly gutsy passage accompanies the final scene of Tyll's decapitation, death and resurrection as a rocky hill: "When the country is in peril again, come and wake me up. I will rise and help my people." Moscow, it seems, was too busy checking the colours to note this rousing call of protest and cry for help. "A small nation must have help," says Arrak, "If we don't believe in God, mythology will help. Or today, NATO – the new Big Tyll."

The film's violent nature – Tyll's sadism as well as the many scenes of mass slaughter, decapitation and bloodshed – attracted criticism from Russia. Raamat was called before many institutions to explain why he used the colour red. A newspaper mocked the film for its use of red on the screen and Arrak's design was heavily criticized. "Blood is blood," laughs Arrak, "It's not milk coming out when a head is cut off!"

In keeping with Moscow's absurdity, *Big Tyll* was, in spite of all the controversy, allowed to screen at many international festivals where it received a number of awards (notably an award at the 1982 Ottawa International Animation Festival in Canada). Those in power must have clearly recognized the artistic quality (not to mention the national sentiment) of the film and decided that it was a good public relations (or in those days, what was called propaganda) move to release the film to international festivals. From afar it would appear as if the Soviet Union was a tolerant society that allowed freedom of expression. But, naturally, the patriotic *Big Tyll* was not something to be shown domestically.

While Raamat was satisfied with the film, the same cannot be said for Arrak. " It was a good experience for me and I am thankful to Rein that he took me to this job but one film was enough for me. I don't like to work with other people. I always see mistakes in my own works ... but when other people are doing it ... I see lines that are not as correct as mine ... It's a good film but there are details missing ... it's like an untuned piano." Arrak was also a little disappointed that he didn't get more credit for his work. "The design was mine and it won prizes at festivals but it was too bad that I didn't have the opportunity of attending. I was just a worker." After *Big Tyll*, Raamat asked Arrak to collaborate on a film version of the famous Estonian national legend, *Kalevpoeg*, but Arrak had had enough animation for his lifetime. Instead,

Raamat turned to another Estonian artist for inspiration, the late Eduard Wiiralt.

Hell is Raamat's most accomplished film. The film is based on three black and white etchings made by Wiiralt between 1930–32 while he was living in Paris. Deeply influenced by the German Expressionism which Wiiralt had absorbed a decade earlier while studying in Dresden, the etchings express the frustrations of wartime, poverty and corruption. In the drawings, Wiiralt depicts human figures in surreal and grotesque caricatures. The first drawing, "Hell" (1930–32), is an anarchistic vision of hell filled with contorted heads branching out of one another, violent mechanical objects, and heads exploding into mushroom clouds. In "Cabaret" (1931), an orgy of grotesques, some well-dressed, and others in rags, dance, drink and flirt. The setting is a strange nightclub populated with dancers, a creepy old violinist and his two naked colleagues who perform atop a massive violin. In the background we see branches with ghoulish souls reaching out. Finally, in "Preacher" (1932), a group of people have gathered around a preacher to hear his warnings of what is to come. "Preacher" contains the same grotesque and surreal images of the previous drawings as well as their powerfully expressionistic flavour. In his film, Raamat merged these three images into one and depicts Wiiralt's drawing in an underground nightclub where people dance, eat, drink, and flirt without limitations, torn between the enticing music of a flute-playing demon and the more soulful, heavenly strings of a maestro's violin. Heaven and hell co-exist in this world, as they do within every one of us. But so too reason. "We can find these three characteristics inside every one of us", says Raamat, "The destructive side of hell is covered over by civilization nowadays – like concrete. So this personal hedonism and lust is regulated within society. And the third characteristic –every person's self-regulator to warn against chaos."

Aside from Lepo Sumera's schizophrenic score and the amazingly detailed re-creation of Wiiralt's the stark expressionistic design of Wiiralt's world, the most striking aspect of *Hell* is Janno Põldma's roller coaster camerawork feverishly panning and zooming throughout the film to create a dizzying, hyper, whirlwind atmosphere. "With Raamat it was quite interesting," says Põldma, "it was creative. He wasn't sure about what he wanted actually and when we made *Hell* he gave me free reign to do what I wanted. So I made all these camera movements, rapid zooms, etc. For me, this was my most interesting work as a cameraman."

Needless to say a stark critique of modern society was bound to

find opposition with the Moscow censors. In fact, Raamat was even told that no one had ever attempted such a film and that it would not be possible to make it. Even after the script was approved, Raamat faced constant interruptions. "I had to sit down with the commissioning editor in Moscow and spend many hours trying to explain the concept of the film. It was a stop-start process, needing much explanation before permission to continue was granted. The only thing that the censors made me include in the film was a reference to the rise of totalitarian states in the thirties – in their minds a reference to Nazi Germany. So I did that, but basically I was happy with what I was able to express." The system had grown extremely rigid by this time and, even after a screenplay had been approved, there was no guarantee that the film would be made.

Actors Kaljo Kiisk and Ülle Toming at movements rehearsal for *Hell*, 1983.

"Raamat's *Hell*," says Sylvia Kiik, "was stopped two or three times during production. What a catastrophe." When Goskino accepted a film, it meant that the film could be shown in the all-union film circuit. This organization was vital for the studios as it provided production funds, but was dependent solely on the basis of Goskino's screenplay approval. If censorship issues halted production, so too the flow of money. "There were two types of control," says Kiik, "ideological and financial. The situation here was that

Rein Raamat, *Hell*, 1983.

Estonian animation frightened Moscow a bit, especially when Raamat created his studio and gathered his group of talented artists. Only then did people understand that you could say a lot in animation." To meet the system everyone learned to be clever: to lie, to pretend, to keep ideas to themselves. "If Goskino really knew what was going on," says Kiik, "these films never would have been made. They didn't understand what *Tyll* was about because they hadn't seen the artistic side of it. Thinking back to that period, I admire the strength of Raamat. *Hell* created a lot of discussion and was strongly attacked by the press and at a certain point it seemed that officials wanted to stop Raamat's work totally."

When Raamat finished the film, one of the Moscow men who told him it was impossible to make such a film congratulated him, further saying that Raamat had made the impossible come true. But completion of a film was no guarantee of exhibition and distribution and *Hell* was shelved for a year until Jean Luc Xiberras of the Annecy Animation festival requested it. "We could not enter films into festivals in those days," says Raamat, "Often it was only afterwards that we were informed that our film had been entered." *Hell* was also shown in Estonia, and even won first prize in the category of artistic film at the Soviet "All-Union" film festival, but was never shown in Soviet cinemas. "With every film I have done, I have had to go through these kinds of processes," says Raamat. It is not clear why *Hell* was banned after winning an award. While one suspects that Raamat's vision of Hell was viewed as a frank critique of the Soviet system, it's also important to realize that many of the Estonians didn't even clearly understand the reasons behind many Moscow decisions. As with *Big Tyll* however, Moscow clearly used *Hell* internationally as a propagandistic showcase of their 'superior' culture.

After *Hell*, Raamat would make only two more films with Joonisfilm: *Kerjus* (The Beggar, 1982) and *Linn* (The City, 1988). Both films display Raamat's interest in injustice and corruption along with his refusal of a single design style.

While here hailing Raamat for his courage and accomplishments within this oppressive system, let's not exaggerate the applause. At its core, Raamat's work is preachy and moralistic, espousing either/or scenarios (man vs. nature, good vs. evil, rich vs. poor) that reduce the often paradoxical nature of reality to a more paint-by-numbers fantasy. Raamat's world is too simple in its critiques and solutions. As Raamat himself has said, "I have tried to express general human ideas that can't possibly be opposed by anyone." Or as Estonian film critic Jaan Ruus suggests, "Raamat is the best example of an Estonian peasant point of view of the world." In short, reality is not as logical and rational as Raamat's art imagines it to be.

When Estonian independence re-emerged in 1991 and Raamat had the opportunity to join his younger colleagues when they re-formed Joonisfilm as a private company, he declined and instead started his own studio, Studio B. The idea was to produce non-violent television shows for children. This labour-intensive endeavour would require a least 120 employees. But, for whatever reason, Tallinnfilm would not allow Raamat to use existing employees. Tallinnfilm had given Raamat access to their lab but he was told that if he borrowed even one employee they would take this privilege away from him. Raamat was therefore forced to hire young, inexperienced staff: "They were all really new except for two brave people" (including Joonisfilm colleague, Avo Paistik). Ironically, many of the then-inexperienced are now working at Joonisfilm and Studio A (a Danish-Estonian service studio).

"I think Studio B was quite a nuisance for many people," says Raamat, "because we were considered a competitor." During the four years the studio survived, Raamat managed to make about twenty-four episodes for two children's series along with another short feature. The Studio closed down when the bank halted funding. The details surrounding the closure are unclear but it is certain that there was competition between Studio B and the new Joonisfilm and only one could survive: the government chose Joonisfilm, somewhat ironically, over Joonisfilm's original founder.

Raamat remains level-headed about the experience: "The freedom to do everything on your own was there then and I was a bit gullible. The opportunities were there but the basis to do them was not."

Some colleagues rolled their eyes at Raamat's ambitions. After years of making state-supported art, Raamat recognized that a new system with new rules was in place. Unfortunately, he lacked the necessary administrative skills needed to survive in this new system, but he at least tried to do something by himself.

When Studio B went bankrupt, Raamat returned to his first love – painting. He also made many documentary films, produced a number of independent films, mostly about Estonian artists, and, in 2000, made an autobiographical documentary film about his experiences as an animator. He is now hoping to find support for a more ambitious film about Eduard Wiiralt.

The Studio B failure left Raamat with a, not entirely unwarranted, bitter taste towards animation. He is also, and this is perhaps less warranted, critical of contemporary films: "If we look at films nowadays the visual style has changed quite a lot and very many of them are too simple. I'm not saying that they are as simple as a traffic sign, but my opinion is that films are for people and they should get something out of it. Otherwise, why make them? I wouldn't be able to do anything like that today. Maybe I'm a bit nostalgic for the old Soviet films because they were professionally made and the message they carried was often good." Perhaps Raamat is simply longing for the days when he was the boss. Along with Sylvia Kiik, Raamat had a lot of power and, according to many animators, he used that power to his advantage and was not the easiest person to work with. Raamat, according to almost everyone, has always lacked a sense of humour, was very anal and seemed to hold grudges for no clear reason. He often failed to recognize the developing talents of his colleagues. As such, people like Mati Kütt and Janno Põldma were not able to make their own films for many years.

Avo Paistick.

But hey, why quibble over hearsay? The truth, as always, is somewhere in the middle. Just as I criticize Raamat's work for its lack of middle ground, then I certainly cannot turn around and reduce him to an either-or figure. Whatever he may have done or not done, it is clear that he paved the way for all of the future Joonisfilm creators. He went out of his way to hire people with good educations and with non-traditional backgrounds like caricature and political cartoons. Furthermore, through his collaborations with Estonian poets, painters and musicians, he opened the doors between many of the art forms while giving voice to the Estonian character in his films. Without Rein Raamat, there quite frankly would be no Priit Pärn, Mati Kütt, Heiki Ernits, or Janno Põldma. And without them, there would be nothing today.

Avo Paistik: From Crayons to Christ

As Joonisfilm became more established and successful, there was pressure on Raamat (as there had been on Elbert Tuganov) to make more films and that meant more directors. The first person to graduate from artist to director was Avo Paistik. "I was asked my opinion," says Raamat, "and I saw that Paistik had ability and talent and I gave my approval. It turns out that I chose the right person."

Avo Paistik was born in Tallinn on 21 April 1936 ("directly between Hitler and Lenin," he notes). His father was a customs officer who was fired after occupation for not teaching the workers to sing 'Internationale'. When World War II started, his father was going to be forced to don a Red Army uniform to defend the new rule. Instead, he fled to the woods. Meanwhile, Paistik's mother felt it was safer to put Avo and his sister, Aasa, into an orphanage. A few years later, their house burned down.

Paistik studied at Industrial school #49, graduating the same year Stalin died (1953). He then studied at the Tallinn Polytechnical School and graduated in 1963 as a radio technician.

Paistik remembers always drawing. Even when he was a Radio Location Officer in the Soviet army, he drew. He liked drawing so much that after he finished his military service he took a course with the Estonian caricature artist, Heinz Valk. "He was an extraordinary teacher," says Paistik.

Paistik's first caricature was published in 1968 in a youth maga-

zine called *Noorus*. Not long after, his caricatures were being accepted in a number of international publications and festivals.

Three Jolly Fellows,
Edgar Valter, Mati Kütt
and Avo Paistick,
1983.

Paistik worked briefly in a military factory before landing a position in 1971 as a senior engineer in Tallinnfilm's audio department. One day he happened to see some animation films that Rein Raamat was projecting. He was intrigued. Within a year, Raamat invited Paistik to work as an animation artist.

This was not actually Paistik's first experience with animation. Prior to that, Paistik was invited by fellow caricaturist Kalju Kurepõld to work on some advertising films he was making for Reklaam films. "We made two films, doing the shooting at night at the Estonian Television studio. The films were quite long and both dealt with traffic safety. Kurepõld taught me how to move the puppets and then went down to have some brandy while I moved them."

Paistik enjoyed working as an artist and didn't relish the hassle of being a director. Both Raamat and Sylvia Kiik had already asked Paistik to direct and he had refused. In 1972, he wrote a script for a film to be called *Pühapäev* (Sunday). "Kiik read it and said it was good. I told them, 'okay, I'll direct a film but only if it's based on my own screenplay.'" But Moscow wanted children's films and there had been a competition to find good screenplays. Paistik was one of the screenplay readers and he liked one called *Värvipliiatsites* (Crayons), but it didn't even cross his mind to direct a film version. "Sylvia Kiik then said to me," remembers Paistik, " 'You did like the screenplay and Moscow wants children's films and won't allow adult films.' I said, 'then I won't direct the film.' One is brave when one has nothing to lose."

The next day Kiik told Paistik he had to see the Tallinnfilm studio director. A man with an "elegant grey suit" invited Paistik in, looked at him squarely from across his large desk and said, "You know Mr. Paistik, I don't know you but be so good as to become a director because all the papers have been submitted to Moscow about you." Paistik said, "Ok." And after that, Paistik, as we shall see, always a tad obsessive with everything he was to do in life, became fixated on being a director and stopped drawing caricatures altogether.

In 1973, Paistik directed his first film, *Crayons*. The film, intended for children, features crayons as the main characters. Using colours symbolically, Paistik tells a humorous tale of a black crayon's disruption of all the beauty created by the yellow, red, and blue crayons. In the end, the crayons are reconciled and the black crayon begins to contribute its own positive images to the surrounding landscape. *Crayons,* despite some fairly obvious symbol-

ism (apparently the Moscow authorities did not like the idea of the black crayon's refusal to cooperate--black being one of the Estonian national colours), is a simple film with modest ambitions.

For the next four years, Joonisfilm followed the two-director system of Nukufilm with Raamat and Paistik each making a new film every year. As with Raamat, there is almost no defining style that can be attributed to Paistik's work. "I never even wanted to copy myself. All of my films are very different." Until the mid 1980s, his films alternated between fairly straightforward, albeit successful, children's work (the three part series *Klaabu* and the feature film *Naksitrallid* (Three Jolly Fellows, 1984) and Zagreb/Pop Art influenced satires like *Täheke* (The Little Star, 1974), *Pisiasi* (A Trifle, 1975), and *Lask* (A Shot, 1976).

The Shot was Paistik's first international success, selected for the Annecy Festival in 1977. However, there were some problems because of Paistik's representation of black men in the film. Elbert Tuganov, who was on the Annecy jury that year, wanted to stop the film from being screened for fear that blacks might riot; a strange sentiment given that you won't find a 'whiter' community than the animation one. Besides, Paistik's depiction is certainly harmless enough. After all, Paistik was a caricaturist and every one of the characters in this satirical film is exaggerated. That's the essence of caricature.

The most interesting of Paistik's early films are *Sunday* and *Tolmuimea* (The Vacuum Cleaner, 1978). In 1977, Paistik finally had the opportunity to make a film from his first script, *Sunday*, a critique of technology in which a man spends his day having everything done for him by technological means. Until then he hadn't been able to get the script approved. He was told that such problems didn't exist in the Soviet Union. Once again, Silvia Kiik came to the rescue. "Silvia helped a lot because the topic was quite suspect. I even wrote into the script that the film was about capitalists to clearly separate it from our world. Then Kiik said, 'it's summertime, all the big bosses are on holiday, and maybe we can deal with the smaller ones.'" Kiik's theory paid off, but just barely. The Moscow editor warned the duo, "I know you Avo Paistik! I know you will change the film and I won't let you do it!" Kiik told her immediate boss of Moscow's reaction but, for whatever reason, he let them make the film. "I wrote a screenplay for myself, a second one for Goskino and a third that would be acceptable to Moscow, but when I made the film it was different from all three scripts!"

Sunday was designed by Priit Pärn and featured music from Pink

Floyd's *Dark Side of the Moon*. After commissioning music from his usual composer, Paistik felt that the music wasn't right. Deadlines were quite strict and with one night to find something appropriate Paistik ended up taking phrases from Pink Floyd's *Money* and *The Great Gig in The Sky*. The music fit the film perfectly. The finished film was well received but it wasn't allowed to screen abroad because of the failure to obtain the rights to the music. Paistik suspects that some internal politics got in the way of a possible festival screening in Stuttgart, Germany. "Someone in Stuttgart wanted the film to appear at the festival yet he never received the application materials. I won't say who but one of our directors went to Moscow and pushed through their film instead."

Avo Paistick, *The Vacuum Cleaner*, 1978.

Much of *Sunday*'s uniqueness stems from its artist. Priit Pärn's consciously 'sloppy', deformed, potato-looking characters coupled with the pop art, and to a lesser degree futurist, inspired backgrounds give the film, for its time anyway, a modern look. More importantly, here was a film dealing with the problems of modern life. There were no animal or crayon symbols. The dehumanizing impact of modernity upon humanity was front and centre. Sure, Paistik told the authorities that the film critiqued capitalist life, but the intended target included modern Estonians. Contrary to what some Westerners might have imagined, Tallinn was no backwater swamp. Western culture, fears, ideas were all accessible in the 1970s. In fact, consumerism reached a high point in Tallinn between 1968–75. Many materials, from exotic foods to washing machines and furniture, became available. Estonians travelled more, television became increasingly popular, and youth culture, heavily influenced by the West, emerged.

Sunday also gives us a taste of what was to come from Priit Pärn. In some ways, *Sunday* is very much a Pärn film. Aside from the obvious visual resemblance, the theme and tone of the film foreshadow some of Pärn's early films. However, the rhythm and overall lack of humour have little in common with Pärn's often absurd and comic sensibilities. Naturally, pinpointing influences is futile (we are influenced by so many little events), but *Sunday* certainly raises the question: Did Priit Pärn add this new modern, ironic sensibility to Paistik's film or did Pärn's own work benefit from his work with Paistik?

Subtlety was never a Paistik amigo. Unlike Pärn, Paistik didn't like to play games with his audience, nor was he as anal as Raamat about formal aesthetics. He had an idea and wanted it clearly articulated and understood. *The Vacuum Cleaner* is a perfect example. A man buys a new vacuum, turns it on, and loses control of it. The vacuum goes on a rampage, first sucking up everything

Avo Paistick, *Jump*, 1985.

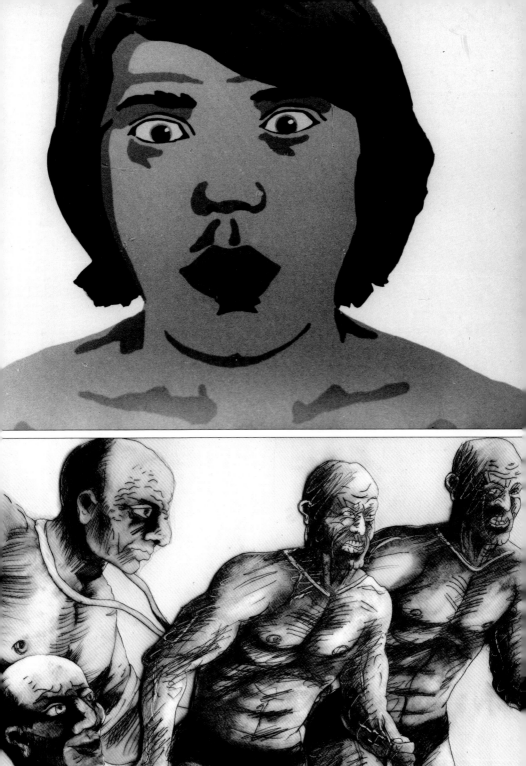

in the house, and then, everything around the house: trees, cows, and homes. All the while, the vacuum grows in size. Finally, the man manages to reach the power button to switch the vacuum off, thereby restoring the area to its previous state. Once again, the influence of pop art, especially Roy Lichtenstein circa 1968 (see "Study for Preparedness"), resonates through the smooth, glossy, metallic visuals of the film.

What's most interesting about it is that the film was even made. And while there is the story about the censors raising a fuss over the vacuum being red (the dominant colour of the Soviet flag), that seems to be a minor concern given that the overall film is condemning those who suck the life from the world (i.e. Russians). And yes ... of course ... you can argue that Paistik was more concerned with modern materialism and that the vacuum represented materialism gone rampant, but this is my book.

Animation filmmaking was a tough process for Paistik: "I wasn't liked very much and with each film I was never sure that I would make another." With almost every film he seemed to have problems. He wrote a screenplay called *Hüpe* (Jump) in 1980 but Moscow refused the go-ahead due to the film's not-so-subtle criticism of the Soviet Union. "The Soviet Union, like Nazi Germany, lured people with ribbons and medals," says Paistik. "This was how they inspired people to be better. But a person becomes wiser with age." But for Paistik the issue was spiritual not political: "It was a biblical film; it was philosophical. But who in those days would allow you to make a film about God?" *Jump* would eventually get made in 1985.

Despite his problems with authorities, Paistik was well liked at Tallinnfilm. "When I knew Paistik," says Priit Pärn, "he was a nice, jovial fatso. He never rejected any pleasures." But by the early 1980s, Paistik was beginning to change. Oddly enough, Pärn may have been the one who inadvertently altered Paistik's life: "I came back from Tartu with my judo coach. He was offering lessons to anyone who wanted to stay fit. I can't remember if I asked Paistik to come, but he came." Paistik, an obsessive person, embraced martial arts and yoga intensely. He began fasting for long periods of time. "I think he lost his way," says Pärn, "and changed his appearance and way of thinking. But I consider it human development."

The change in Paistik's life is very clearly reflected in his Bergmanesque trilogy of films: *Jump* (1985), *Lend* (Flight, 1988), and *Silmus* (Noose, 1989). The colour, irony, humour, and innocence of his previous work are replaced by bleak, expressionistic, charcoal drawings. Gone are the frivolities of modern humanity as Paistik turns his attention to the larger issues of spiritual emptiness and redemption. In all three films, achingly alienated characters struggle against all manner of obstacles to find harmony and peace. For the re-born Paistik, this serenity could only be found in God.

With censorship in the Soviet Union fading in the post-Brezhnev era, Paistik was finally able to make *Jump*, the best of his religious trilogy. *Jump* is a sublime critique of the folly of over-reaching in which a man is broken by the very world that he has created. In the film, a baby's first steps gradually evolve into walking, and running, and then into a man's hurdle-jumping conquests. Rather than experiencing satisfaction at what he has accomplished, he pursues new and more difficult hurdles. But with each new hurdle, higher expectations are placed upon him. Finally, the man literally cracks after he has jumped his last hurdle. Living in the moment rather than for the moment, the protagonist watches life run by, unlived.

Jump was an international success, winning awards at various festivals including Stuttgart, Germany ("I won 3000 deutch-marks, but [after the bureaucrats took their cut] only received a very small amount of rubles!") and Kiev, where it received an astounding four prizes.

After the trilogy, Paistik would make only one more film – appropriately titled *Minek* (The Departure, 1990). By the time of independence, Paistik was heavily into painting and God. "I couldn't go on with Joonisfilm," says Paistik, "I was already into God and couldn't divert myself. I was offered a chance to make religious films in Moscow with an unlimited budget, but I decided that even under these conditions I wasn't able to make films." Paistik continues to receive invitations to Estonian animation screenings, but never accepts.

However, Paistik did accept an invitation from Rein Raamat to work at Studio B. However, after it became clear that Raamat was unwilling to share any authority with his long-time colleague, Paistik left the studio. Paistik's last involvement with animation concerned a rather strange project initiated by a millionaire who had asked Paistik to make a feature film. A script was written ("a very good screenplay," notes Paistik) and there ended the initiative.

Paistik remains a ferocious painter. His studio is filled with oil paintings, of a mostly religious nature. "I haven't seen any animation films in the last 10 years," says Paistik, "I don't even have a television." Paistik also stopped doing caricatures long ago: "I've been invited by magazines, but I can't think in that direction anymore."

Religion now dominates every aspect of Paistik's life. When I visited his studio in March 2002, he showed me his Bible. It was well-used and almost every page was littered with highlighted passages. Paistik spreads his beliefs through a Christian radio show and as a preacher at an Estonian church: "I am telling the people what the church has failed to tell them."

"Gradually I started to understand that other people didn't know what I knew," says Paistik, "I didn't believe it at first. I even left the Pentecostal church because I was teaching those who had taught me. I have to act according to the Bible, but why don't other people want to follow it?"

Chapter Six

Estonia Catches Up With Modern Art

While the founding of Nukufilm coincided with the rise of modern art in Estonia, one would be hard pressed to find its stamp in the works of Tuganov, Raamat, or Pars. However, the absurd, grotesque, surrealist and, to a lesser degree, pop art leanings of Avo Paistik and, as we shall see, of Priit Pärn and of almost every artist that followed him, would clearly not have been possible without the 'thaw' in the arts of the post-Stalin era of the late 1950s and 1960s.

Growing up in a more culturally liberal post-Stalin Estonia, Pärn and colleagues had access to increasing amounts of Western art and thought (which had really been cut off from 1940–1957 or so). As the Soviet Union's cultural policies began to 'thaw' in the late 1950s, foreign literature began to filter through to Estonia. Translations of Beckett, Kafka, Brecht and other influential writers became available by 1957 and, by the late 1960s, Polish and Czech art magazines also appeared. In the 1960s, Estonian art began to reflect international trends. A number of radical artists like Leonard Lapin, Ulo Sooster, and Tonis Vint inspired a generation of Estonians and Russians with their Soviet Pop art, surrealist exhibits and manifestos. As Anu Livvak notes, "[In the 1960s], Estonian art experienced, somewhat covertly, most of the ideas of 20th century art." This artistic explosion expanded beyond art – into literature, theatre, music (Arvo Pärt) and, eventually, animation.

The rapid influx of Western thought into Estonia was due primarily to its fortuitous geographical location. Owing to Estonia's proximity to Finland, access to Western culture (mostly through Finnish television, which was available as early as 1961) was easier to come by than for other Soviet republics. At the same time, Estonia's distance from Moscow made it impossible to harness or censor these transitions. In the end, Estonia was afforded a measure of freedom that was not possible in other parts of the Soviet Union.

Soviet occupation had a negative effect on artistic development in Estonia. If it wasn't socialist realist art, then, hey, it wasn't art. All forms of 'alternative' art were relegated to obscurity. Incredibly, this harsh censorship led many Estonian artists to be more resolute in their search for self-expression. From Stalin's death onwards, artists quietly held exhibitions in studios, clubs and even the homes of their friends and relatives. Some even had their work exhibited abroad.

Modern art in post-WWII Estonia starts with Ulo Sooster. He studied at the Pallas art school in Tartu. (Pallas was coldly renamed "The Art Institute" by the Soviets.) The Pallas school had been in existence for about thirty years at this time and its teachers included many of Estonia's leading painters. Sooster graduated from "Pallas" in 1949. Before the year was out, he was arrested and sentenced to ten years in a prison camp for associating with an anti-Soviet group. Ironically, it was during his prison years that Sooster really developed as an artist. He did a number of self-portraits and drawings depicting the stagnant, mundane life of prison. Sooster's expressionistic, autobiographical paintings were an anomaly in Estonian art, where classical painting, with its restrained emotions, had dominated for so long.

After his release from prison, Sooster married Lidia Serh (a big influence on his life and art) and, as settling in Estonia was not an option, they moved to Moscow. In Moscow, Sooster's art flourished. His work went through a variety of phases: from the highly erotic to the Picasso-influenced and finally the adoption of surrealism and abstraction. By the mid 1960s Sooster had become the leader of Unofficial Soviet Art. His originality motivated and awed both younger and older colleagues. Sooster's life was cut short in Moscow in 1970 under suspicious circumstances.

It's of course ironic that the man who kick-started modern art in Estonia spent most of his life abroad (not unlike Estonia's leading artist of the pre-War period, Eduard Wiiralt), but throughout his life in Moscow, Sooster maintained close ties with Estonian artists and was the prime instigator behind the formation of two art groups in Estonia.

Around 1958, a number of Tartu artists, who had studied at Pallas

with Sooster, had begun to have informal underground exhibitions of their own. Sooster was responsible for bringing most of the artists together. Their work was quite diverse in technique and concept, but was largely influenced by abstract collage, surrealism and pop art. This group of artists were bonded together by their desire to express themselves on their own terms. Probably the most important event of this unofficial group's history was an exhibition at a Tartu secondary school in 1960. The exhibition sparked a hostile reaction from the authorities and the paintings were criticized severely for their un-realist tendencies. Reception aside, the Tartu exhibition signalled the birth of the first post-war art group in Estonia. The group (of course, they did not call themselves a group) continued experimenting throughout the 1960s. The group was disbanded in the early 1970s and artists continued on their own paths. The group's biggest historical impact was its very existence. It kept ties to the older Pallas alive and, with that, to Estonian art traditions, while simultaneously introducing new concepts into Estonian art circles. The "Pallas" group also quietly ushered in the evolution of Estonia's second art group, ANK.

"In 1964," says Estonian painter, Juri Arrak, "our group of students, ANK, had a secret exhibition in one room of a theatre in Estonia. It was officially forbidden." The student group included Arrak, Aili Vint (who was the art director on Rein Raamat's *Flight*), and Tõnis Vint, who became the leader of this newgeneration of artists.

Like the Pallas group, ANK was less concerned with making political statements against the Soviet Union than it was about freedom of personal expression. "Our history stopped at the 20th century," says Arrak, "There was no cubism or surrealism. In Leningrad, I secretly read about modern artists like Kandinsky and Malevitš. Our group of artists wanted to catch up. There had been a gap of 20 years due to the Soviets. We wanted exposure to those artistic models and to things that existed in Western Europe so we could jump over the gap and start doing the things ourselves."

Beyond libraries, Estonian artists learned about art through Polish, Czech and Hungarian art magazines. "And some books came to us," adds Arrak, "through Estonian emigrés who visited us. I met our friends in Canada and Sweden and they brought art books. They were like a treasure and we passed them around to each other. There is a good library at Tartu University. It was no problem."

One of those who was not part of the group, but was strongly influenced by Vint, was Leonard Lapin. Leonard Lapin enrolled at the Tallinn Art Institute in 1966. Lapin, like the other students, educated himself in 20th century art, theory, literature, psychology, and philosophy.

In 1969, Lapin (who by the 1970s was the most radical of the Estonian avant-garde), along with fellow artists Andres Tolts and Ando Keskküla, started a group called *Soup*. (The name was indebted to Andy Warhol) Here were the roots of Pop Art (or Soviet Pop as it was called) in Estonia. And if there is an obvious link between Estonian art and animation, that link is certainly Soviet Pop. It proved influential on the Lapin-designed *Wonderbird* by Rein Raamat and a number of early Avo Paistik films including *The Little Star*, *Sunday*, and *The Vacuum Cleaner*. In fact, Keskküla made two animation films – *Lugu Jänesepojast* (The Story of Little Rabbit, 1975) and *Jänes* (Rabbit, 1976) – with Joonisfilm.

This artistic re-awakening was not limited to the medium of graphic arts. In 1957, the library of Looming (Loomingu Raamatukogu) began publishing translations of Beckett, Brecht, and Kafka, among others. The influence of these writers can be found in the absurd leanings of Estonian theatre of the 1960s and undoubtedly crept into the political caricatures of artists like Priit Pärn.

While much of Estonian literature remained largely unimpressive, a few authors distinguished themselves during this time, such as Jaan Kross. Primarily historical, his books focus on reclaiming Estonian figures of the past (two have been translated into English: *The Czar's Madman*, *Professor Marten's Departure*). But while Kross was more rooted in traditional realist forms of expression, modernism also found its way into Estonian literature via short story writers Arvo Valton and Mati Unt. Not surprisingly, both authors, in their use of the absurd, grotesque, existential and psychological, were influenced by the Estonian translations of Beckett and Kafka.

Poetry also evolved from the didactical crap of earlier times into something more lyrically inspired. Jaan Kaplinski and Paul-Eerik Rummo (who, you will remember, scripted two animation films for Rein Raamat) were among the many significant poets to emerge.

And finally, Estonian music (to be discussed in more detail later) offered two important new composers: Veljo Tormis, who re-interpreted many traditional Estonian songs in a new choral format, and, perhaps the most famous Estonian in the world right now, Arvo Pärt, who began his journey towards spiritual minimalism in the 1960s through experimentation with modernist techniques. Pärt also scored many animation films for both Nukufilm and Joonisfilm.

Aside from national creativity, equally important in the 1960s were access to Finnish Television and the increase in visiting artists. Because of Estonia's proximity, Finnish TV was often available in Estonian homes. As former Estonian President Lennart Meri said, "When the television broadcasts started on Finnish TV, we were out of the Soviet Union. We were with the rest of the world when Armstrong took the first steps on the moon. We were there with you when President Kennedy was shot. We knew what was going on outside the Iron Curtain. What we didn't know was the smell of a fresh banana."

Finnish TV provided Estonians with a window onto the rest of the world. Estonians were able to see what the West had and what they didn't have. But, less materially, they were exposed to a wide range of cultural forms of expression through news programs, sitcoms, dramas and films.

Not only did Estonian artists have their work exhibited abroad at film, art, music and caricature festivals throughout the sixties, but a number of exhibitions took place in Tallinn. More specific to animation, French, German, British (John Halas, Bob Godfrey), Bulgarian (Todor Dinov), and Yugoslavian (Borivoj Dovnivic) animators all made visits to Tallinn to show their work.

Naturally, this was by no means a detailed account (political cartoons and caricatures had an enormous influence on post-1960s Estonian animators) of what must have been an exciting time in Estonia. This chapter was merely intended as a quick overview providing some barebones socio-cultural context for the next generation of Estonian animators.

The generation of Estonian animators who grew up in the 1960s (Priit Pärn, Janno Põldma, Mati Kütt, Heiki Ernits) and 1970s (Rao Heidmets, Harvi Volmer, Riho Unt, Kalju Kivi) came of age in a very different and relatively more open Estonia than the previous generation of Tuganov, Pars and Raamat. The work of this new generation, with its grotesque, surrealist, absurd, playful, and increasingly personal expression, is in different ways a reflection of the 1960s artistic re-awakening.

Chapter Seven

Fat Chicks and Imbeciles

Aside from being the poster boy for Estonian animation, Priit Pärn is one of the animation world's greatest gifts to the eyes and ears. An illegitimate cross-breeding of George Grosz, Monty Python and Jean-Luc Godard, Pärn's works are often bitingly funny, complex, self-reflective explorations of the effects of social, political and economic systems on human beings. In laymen's terms: how people live.

Pärn's films have received roaring applause and fancy trophies from a variety of festivals, but more meaningful has been Pärn's far-reaching impact on both Estonian and international animation. In addition to his films, Pärn has a long history as a creator of 'children's' books, as a noted graphic artist, as a teacher at Turku Film Academy in Finland, and as a guest lecturer internationally. Pärn's renown has brought students from as far afield as Finland, Switzerland, Japan, and recently, America, to Estonia to learn the magical, mystical ways of this man whose name means something like 'lime' in English.

The Pärn 'phenomenon' has even reached the tinselled, plastic shores of California via a few relocated Ruskies and a Ukrainian. Through the hazy, lazy dim light of their Mexican-assembled, American-fed life-boxes, mom and pop and the kiddies can sit back and savour glimpses of the jagged, uneven palette and informal sketchy designs that characterize the Pärn 'style' in such revolutionary fare as *Duckman*, *Rugrats* and *Ahhh Real Monsters*.

Priit Pärn grew up in the town of Tapa, but first saw light inside four poorly painted greyish-white walls somewhere within the Danish-named Estonian centre of Tallinn. It was late in the summer of 1946. While the world cleaned up a landscape of corpses lost in a battle for the pockets of privilege, two rogues with absurd facial hair destroyed Estonian independence.

Beyond the Russian bombings which decimated its people and

buildings, Tapa was a land of railways, a Soviet military aerodome, and little else. But it was home for Rudolf Pärn, a railway worker, his wife, Helene-Rosalie and their two children, Lehte and Priit. The parents were caring, liberal folks who encouraged their children to follow their own paths. For the older Lehte, healing the physical wounds of humanity would be her calling, while Priit went deeper inside, first through biology, later through celluloid, to explore the internal scars of a people whose history was peppered with rape and butchery by foreign fortune seekers.

Priit Pärn.

The road from Tapa to Tallinn is not so long, maybe 50 kilometres, but Pärn would travel down others before finally heading towards his birthright in 1976. Between those years, Pärn pursued a career in biology. He worked as a biologist in the botanical garden in Tallinn as part of a team studying plant ecology.

Thanks to his mother, however, who dabbled in drawing, Pärn inherited a need to draw. While at school he published his first caricature, thereby discovering a means of increasing his cash flow. During his years as a biologist, soldier, husband, father and, even briefly, as a sambo-taught (Russian judo) stuntman (he even appeared as a stuntman in Estonia's most beloved feature film, *The Last Relic*), Pärn drew and drew and drew – sometimes for children, sometimes for adults, but mostly for himself. Unfortunately, his early drawings were not very good. This awareness of his limitations led to his minimalist style: "I understood that my drawing was weak. I had to simplify it. I made the human beings in my drawings more like signs, with very simple lines. Step by step the drawings got better and better." His style was social, absurd, and filled with dark humour. His drawings were published in Tartu and Tallinn newspapers and in magazines. "In those days, there was a daily in Tartu," says Pärn, "which ran a humour section twice a week. My pictures were there every time."

His work confused everyone. Cartoonists were supposed to draw about plumbing problems or be critical of the evil Americans. Pärn's work irritated those who made decisions because, most of the time, they didn't understand what the hell he was expressing. But it wasn't really his problem. If there was trouble, it was the editor's head that rolled. "The border was separating the acceptable from the non-acceptable," says Pärn, "and over time you learned where it was. There was no point drawing pictures that you knew would not be published."

As with animation, festivals were also important in the caricature world: "If your picture was accepted, then the best thing was to win a prize. But, either way, you got a catalogue of the exhibition

and that enabled you to see what was happening around the world."

As it was forbidden to transport works of art outside of the Soviet Union, some innovation was required. An artist's first option was to secure a paper from the Minister of Culture stating that the work was not in fact a work of art. When that failed, there was the post office. "Sending letters wasn't easy," says Pärn, "Often, after a few days, you'd get a notice saying that there is something for you from Belgium and it was just your picture being returned." Sometimes Pärn just posted the picture again, but later discovered that if you sent your package from a smaller village it was more likely to reach its destination. Pärn, always the sportsman, would occasionally ask Finnish sport coaches if they would mail his drawings from Finland.

Caricatures were important to Pärn during his school years because they effectively doubled his earnings. When he became a biologist the money was appreciated, but not so important: "I didn't do caricatures for the money but it was nice to get money for them."

Pärn got so much pleasure from drawing that he made a decision around 1976 to abandon biology. "It was a risky decision," says Pärn, "because during Soviet occupation you could easily be banned from publishing." Parn's biology team was always short of money for their expeditions and while computer technology was available, getting access was quite difficult. More to the point, the repetitive and intricate nature of the job became too much for Pärn. "We developed mathematical models for plants. A square metre was divided into twenty smaller squares. We picked up every plant and determined their species. Then we burned them and tested the ashes to analyse their chemical ingredients. If you spend ten hours a day looking at these plants," says Pärn, "there comes a point when enough is enough."

Pärn had been interested in animation as early as 1972. He'd read a 'help wanted' ad that Joonisfilm had run, but didn't feel he was quite ready for the work. Pärn's exposure to animation was limited to Russian children's films and other "very boring" works. However, in 1972 he attended a seminar on animation in Moscow where he discovered Polish animation: "This was quite interesting. They had strange stories and more art films."

Pärn first met Rein Raamat on the set of *The Last Relic*, where Raamat had been working as an artist. A few years later, the two met again and Raamat invited Pärn to come to Tallinnfilm and have a look around.

"Raamat suggested," says Pärn, "that I make a design for *The*

Gothamites (1974)." Pärn accepted the offer and, along with Estonian artist Kaarel Kurismaa, worked on drawings and suggested a few ideas for Raamat's film, which was based on a story by F.R. Kreutzwald, the author of *Kalevipoeg*.

After turning his back on biology, Parn decided to try animation. Having established contacts in animation through the Moscow seminar, Pärn was invited by Raamat to be a director in the Joonisfilm division (cel animation). At the time, there were only two directors: Raamat and Avo Paistik. However, with a demanding production schedule of 40 minutes, more directors were obviously required. Before Pärn could direct, he had to learn the process. His apprenticeship involved working as an artist on Avo Paistik's *Sunday*. "With Raamat, I walked in, presented my ideas and drawings and walked out again, whereas with Paistik the relationship was less official. Paistik was very open to new ideas," recalls Pärn. "He was the sort of person who could arrive in the middle of the night by taxi because he had a great idea. Of course, in the morning, it often turned out that it wasn't such a good idea!" The biggest obstacle faced by Pärn in his new career was solving technical problems. "I was doing things in time now, so it wasn't just an issue of how the image looked anymore, but rather how it unfolded. This was a new challenge for me."

Pärn was given the chance to direct his own film in 1977. Unlike his later films, the premise of *Is The Earth Round?* is fairly straightforward. A young man travels solely in one direction to prove that the earth is round. "It was like my own problem," says Pärn, "because up to a certain point in my life my main interest was to go as far as I can go through travel. It seemed to me that this was real life. This man opts to leave. His friends have stayed, and now have nice houses. The man returns poor and alone but he has seen the whole world."

While you can see the primitive roots of Pärn's design, colour, playful use of symbolism, and black humour, *Is The Earth Round?* displays the problems of a first film. "At the time, I didn't know anything about film-making," says Pärn. " When we recorded sound I had to think ahead how it would be, to whether it was okay to have some breaks in sound, or whether this was a mistake. It was like inventing a bicycle. I didn't know anything about editing. And, at the same time, I think that this was a good education because I had to trust myself."

In the world of Rein Raamat (which was under the watchful eye of Russian animator, Fedor Khitruk) the boundaries of animation were limited. Each frame had to be pristinely drawn and the motion smooth and realistic. Pärn immediately stood out against the conservative natures of both Raamat and Khitruk. In Moscow animation, everything was Disney; Soyutzmultfilm, Eisenstein and Khitruk loved Walt and his tender tales of innocents wandering through a harsh, evil world towards maturity and heterosexual love. Not surprisingly, the Russians spent the century trying to simulate Walt and his workers. With this in mind, it's easy to understand why Pärn's work, which exhibited a crude drawing style and garish colours, did not please either Raamat or Khitruk.

In fact Khitruk loudly and dismissively referred to Pärn's film as nothing but moving graphics. "I remember where we talked about it – in a screening room," says Pärn, "[Khitruk] said my film style wasn't right and I argued that it was. I think I surprised him. The behaviours in Moscow and in Estonia were quite different. People in lower positions were not supposed to counter those in higher positions. Khitruk was a famous filmmaker and nobody probably ever said to him, 'what I'm doing is okay, this is my film'."

Needless to say Pärn's behaviour created more than its share of tension between Khitruk and the Estonian animators: "I think that Khitruk maybe took things too seriously. You can't treat people like slaves to make your films."

Pärn's willingness to confront Raamat and Khitruk was made possible by the biology career that he could resume: "In the first year I thought that maybe I could go back to biology, but then, step by step, I began to feel that maybe I could survive as a cartoonist. So I took a risk."

To make matters worse, Moscow authorities, accustomed to fairy tales, immediately questioned the film's meaning. "They didn't understand the point of the film," says Pärn, "The story was just a structure." The end result was that while *Is The Earth Round?* was permitted to screen in Estonia, it was banned in the rest of the Soviet Union. "This was very bad for my next film, since the studio didn't like me. But it also made a name for me. If your film is banned for being very bad, then people think that there must be something behind it."

When Pärn began his second film, *And Plays Tricks*, he faced a barrage of problems from Moscow authorities that bore more resemblance to a Monty Python skit than an animation production. First, Pärn was told that his script (about a young bear who annoys the other animals with his tricks) was bad. He persisted, returning every few weeks with a variation of the story. Many re-writes later, the script received approval, but Pärn, deviously, made the film based on his original version of the story. "It was a big risk," notes Pärn, "If I was caught, it would definitely be my last film. Two thirds of the film were completed when production

Priit Pärn, *And Plays Tricks*, 1978.

Priit Pärn, *Triangle*, 1982.

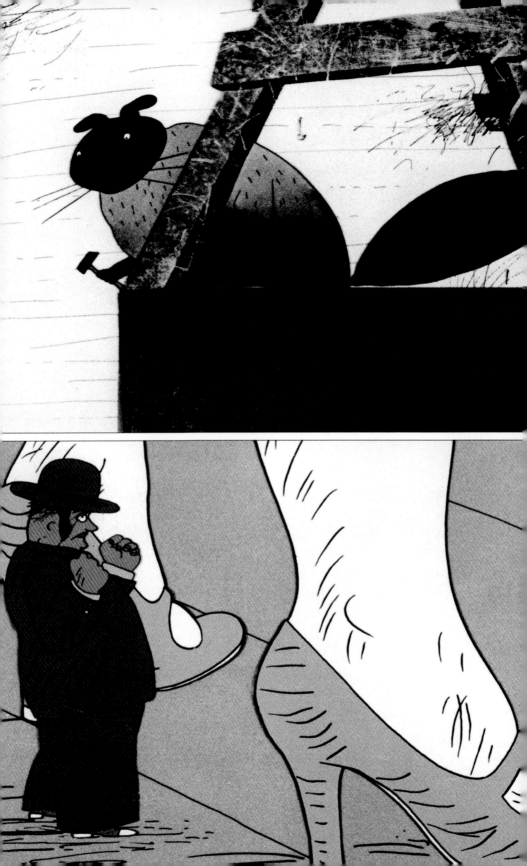

PÄRN 87

was stopped. I was told that I had to devise a new ending. In Russia at this time you had two possibilities: either you said no to changes and your script went into the garbage or you changed the script. So I wrote a new ending. It was actually the best version. I had to cut out a few things, but it was quite okay."

And Plays Tricks was Parn's first international success garnering an award for Best Children's Film at the 1978 Varna Festival. Pärn, who was at the festival, was not able to accept the award. As was typical, that honour went to an anonymous Moscow bureaucrat.

Following *Exercises for an Independent Life,* an interesting film that contrasts the lives of a young boy and an older bureaucrat in order to examine generational conflict, but perhaps more significantly, the loss of imagination, freedom, and innocence as one ages, Pärn made *Kolmnurk* (Triangle, 1982). *Triangle* is considered a landmark in Estonian animation for its examination of modern relations between a man and a woman. Fusing the personal and the political, *Triangle* is a witty commentary of contemporary domestic politics.

Triangle deals with a twisted love triangle between a married couple (Victor and Julia) and the little man who lives under their stove (Eduard). Victor and Julia lead a routine life. She cooks. He reads the paper. Lurking beneath this static relationship are Julia's fantasies of being loved and caressed. When Victor leaves, little Eduard answers Julia's longings for passion and escape. But soon the passion dwindles and Eduard settles comfortably, paper in hand, into Victor's old chair. When Victor returns, there is a brief, joyous moment of reconciliation with Julia, but lust once again turns to sterility and silence. In the meantime, Eduard returns to the stove and his own empty relationship with Veronica, the woman he left behind. Foreshadowing virtually all of Pärn's later films, the characters in *Triangle* are too busy imagining who they are not rather than being who they are.

Pärn has a simpler explanation: "My wife was in the hospital and I was learning how to cook. There is an old Estonian folk tale about a small man who comes out from under the stove, asks for food and then eats everything. I just wanted to make a film about cooking."

Pärn's blunt portrait of domestic life in the Soviet Union was far removed from the typical children's films that were being tossed out in both Estonia and Russia, and it was a shock to many. Igor Kovalyov (*Rugrats: The Movie*), a transplanted Ukrainian who brought Pärn's style to Hollywood, saw *Triangle* in a movie

theatre in Kiev in 1982: "It was playing in front of a live-action feature. I was so amazed that I bought tickets for the next screening just to see *Triangle* again... I had never seen anything like this. I was so excited I called all my friends to find out who this Pärn was."

"No one wanted to allow *Triangle* onto Soviet screens," recalls Estonian film critic Jaan Ruus, "It was controversial among Soviet animators who were used to either drawing like Disney or drawing very exact and precise pictures."

By the mid-1980s, as Glasnost and Perestroika emerged under Mikhail Gorbachev, censorship policies lightened. Furthermore, relatively stable funding was coming from Moscow. For Pärn, the period became a "Golden Age of Estonian animation."

If there is one film that is emblematic of this new period it is *Eine Murul* (Breakfast on The Grass, 1988). *Breakfast on the Grass* is considered by many to be one of the masterpieces of animation. In depicting a few moments in the daily lives of four Estonians, Pärn trenchantly critiques the absurdities of Communist society by giving viewers a rare glimpse of the daily endurance needed to survive in the Soviet Union. As with *Triangle*, *Breakfast on the Grass's* frank portrait of modern Soviet life astonished Soviet audiences.

"I think the general audience was not prepared for this kind of animation," recalls Pärn, "It is a description of a very concrete society told in a realistic way using a dramatic structure that is closer to a live-action feature. But the story is performed using the tools of animation – visual gags, metamorphosis and different drawing styles. Usually so-called serious stories are dark, heavy, slow and boring. I try to make a serious film funny, multileveled and ironic. I think this fusing of the serious and comic confused people."

Breakfast on The Grass is not only an exceptional film because of its content and style; but also because of Pärn's perseverance in realizing his vision. It took Pärn four years to obtain permission to make the film, and even then, once the film was approved, there was no guarantee that it would be ever seen. But it quickly won many major awards and is now heralded as a masterpiece. The premise of *Breakfast* is relatively simple. Four protagonists and five chapters divide the film. Anna wants to buy apples. George wants fine clothing. Berta wants to re-discover her identity, and Eduard, it seems, wants a key. The fifth and final chapter unites the characters to share a brief moment of happiness depicting characters in Manet's famous painting, *Déjeuner sur l'herbe*.

The four characters must overcome a variety of barriers to attain what they want, and Pärn uses their search to criticize Soviet life.

We are introduced to a grey, ugly, paranoid world filled with absurdities and cruelties. One of Pärn's great comic moments, for example, occurs when George attempts to buy a nice suit. He offers money to the tailor but is told that the tailor wants glasses as compensation. George goes to an optician but is told that the optician wants boots. He goes to the cobbler, but the cobbler wants bread. And on and on it goes until, after a relentless search, George finally gets a smart suit.

The suffering is not just individual but collective. Pärn suggests this shared suffering through a number of intersecting images. In each chapter, we see or hear the crash of a taxicab followed by resonant screams. A second link is the figure of Picasso, who is seen in each chapter being hauled away by authorities. Picasso and Manet's presence extends the suffering, not only beyond the individual but also beyond the present. Life under the Soviet system is not the first to cause suffering, nor will it likely be the last.

While the film is dedicated to the "artists who went as far as they were allowed," one senses that this tribute includes the general population who similarly ventured as far as they could within a suffocating system. *Breakfast on The Grass*, while politically and culturally specific, carries with it a timelessness that is both personal and universal. It is this unique interaction between the personal and the collective that makes this one of Pärn's finest and most important films to date.

In 1991, Estonia became an independent country and, once again, Pärn weighs in with the prescient *Hotel E*, a bitter critique of the hypocrisy of both the East and West. While the East represses art and language, he contends, the West, for all its freedom, lacks art and language and, consequently, individuality. Playing with stereotypes, Pärn paints the East as a dark, grey world while filling the West with bright colours and friendly, smiling faces. Beneath this pop-art sugar-coating, he seems to be saying, the West is a culture of sterility and illusion. No one does anything, no ones says anything, yet everything is, as one character continually repeats, "just great."

"I had been traveling a lot between East and West," says Pärn, "I was between two systems. *Hotel E* is my own story – up to a certain point. This is not a film about two systems, about East and West; for me, it is a story about this person." While Estonia's independence afforded Pärn more freedom, it came with a price: "Under the Soviets everything which was not permitted was forbidden. So there were endless restrictions that were political, and just insane. Now all the limits are connected with money. The final result is often the same as before, sometimes worse."

A major weakness in *Hotel E* is Pärn's criticism of the West, and Americans in particular. He lumps Americans into a group of staid, hollow shells who have nothing to do and nothing to say. Now, yes, Parn is exaggerating Western lifestyle to a degree in cautioning Estonian and Soviet viewers not to be too hopeful about the dissolution of the Soviet Union. Still, Pärn's caricature of the West is extreme and relentless. In doing so, he ends up mirroring the perceived hateful and superficial tendencies and attitudes of Americans.

Pärn's post-independence films still contain healthy doses of absurdism and symbolism, but their tone is significantly lighter and wittier. His most recent films, *1895* (co-directed with Janno Põldma in 1995) and *Night of the Carrots*, move beyond examinations of individuals within specific ideological systems toward their positions within larger political-technological infrastructures.

In *1895*, Pärn used the centenary of cinema as an opportunity to deconstruct it. (The film opens with the statement "The cinema, it is a lie.") The structure of the film is straightforward: The protagonist, Jean-Paul, does not know who he is and decides to travel around the world in search of his identity. (It turns out he's the co-creator of cinema, Louis Lumière.)

Pärn uses Jean-Paul's journey to analyze the cinema's influence on our perceptions of the world. Pärn argues that our ideas of nationality and history are constructed by cinema. (For example, footage from Sergei Eisenstein's fictional film *October* was often presented as documentary footage of the Russian Revolution.) Throughout Jean-Paul's travels, each country is reduced to a stereotype: Italy is red wine and the Mafia; Switzerland is clocks and Swiss Army knives.

Cinema, Pärn proposes, has become such a mediating presence that pop-cultural memory often clouds the reality of the past. In a sense, *1895* is an anti-cinema film. It reminds us of a time when motion pictures did not exist and suggests that a movieless world was not such a bad thing. In a world without films, cinema aficionados might have pursued goals more beneficial for humanity. (At one point we learn that François Truffaut was working on the invention of synthetic rain clouds before giving it all up to become a film critic and director.)

As with all of Pärn's work, there is an autobiographical element to *1895*. He acknowledges his own complicity in propagating the evils of cinema through the character of Louis' brother Auguste Lumière, who disappears at the beginning of the film to become a biologist (like Pärn) and returns at the end to invent cinema with

Priit Pärn,
Karl and Marilyn,
2003.

Louis/Jean-Paul. Pärn thereby reverses cinema's role as an instigator of generic memory and instead uses it to explore his personal
memories of both his life and his films.

Pärn's most recent film, 1998's *Night of the Carrots,* examines the
effect of computers and the internet on contemporary society, as
well as the cult of celebrity. The story finds crowds of people, led
by the protagonist, Diego, trying to get into a sanatorium-like
institution called "PGI." It's not clear why these people want in
to PGI; as the narrator says, "Being contenders was their real aim
because once they were in they would have nothing to do." In
each of PGI's rooms we meet a variety of bizarre characters who
want only to escape. The occupants each have personal dreams
that, they soon discover, they cannot realize because they are
literally plugged into their rooms.

Escape from PGI is possible only during one night – when all the
rabbits (who control the world through computers) turn into
carrots. Contrary to the ominous warnings about a Y2K cataclysm
that preceded the new millennium, Pärn instead saw the period
during which he was making *Night of the Carrots* as a moment of
temporary liberation. For one evening, Pärn suggests, we could
step outside of our rooms, away from our computers, embrace
the natural world and, with it, ourselves.

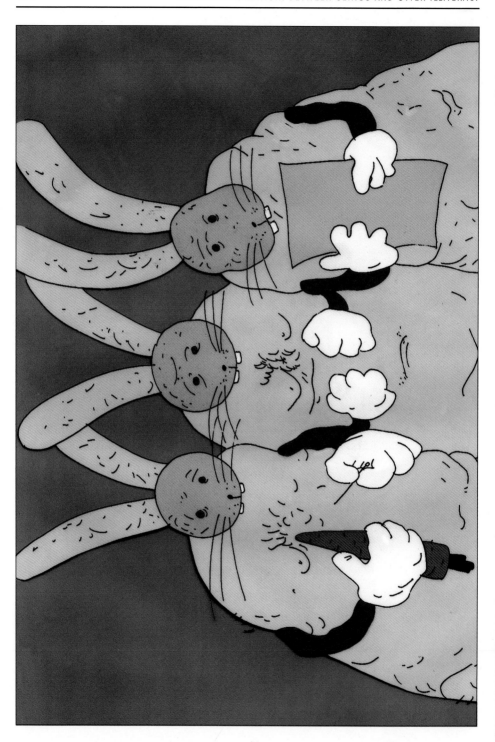

Priit Pärn,
The Night of the Carrots, 1998.

Pärn used his main characters in *Night* – each based on a famous individual – to examine the cult of celebrity. Just as the Internet offers virtual interaction and experience, within PGI's seemingly glamorous world of fame, there is nothing but loneliness and longing.

Pärn's most recent film, *Karl and Marilyn*, is a story about a man and a woman. Karl wants to flee from the pressures of fame. Marilyn, a rural girl, is tired of her boring country life and wants fame. Karl (Marx?) has his beard shaved off, murders the barber, and goes underground. Marilyn (Monroe) kills her grandmother, and goes to the city in search of fame. She achieves it when a gust of wind from the sewer lifts her skirt up. The masses are enthralled. After a while, though, they tire of her skirt antics. During a performance, Karl inadvertently rises out of the sewer. The people are relieved that Karl has returned. Is this a cautionary tale about the return of communism? Are young Estonians rejecting their roots (in one scene, Marilyn is shown knitting with her grandmother in a distinctly Estonian style) for the glitter and glam of capitalism? What happens when they realize just how empty it all is? Will communism (as we're beginning to see hints of in Russia) return to power?

For the record, Pärn thinks this interpretation is ridiculous. "It's a story about a man and woman and how men are always pressured to be someone, while women are simply supposed to 'be'."

Karl and Marilyn is strikingly designed and features some funny moments, but overall the film feels rushed and unsatisfactory.

Beyond his personal films, Pärn has also made a handful of unique commercials over the years. The commercials, all featuring the Pärn 'look' and his sexually-tinged humour, allowed Pärn to be a bit more playful. They include the cider commercial *Oiva* (2000), *Remix* (1999), and a social awareness short for MTV Europe's *Free Action* series (1999). But the best of the bunch remain the controversial *Absolut Pärn* (1996) and the award-winning *Switch off The Lights* (1988).

The Absolut piece was commissioned for a series of online animations to promote Absolut Vodka. The only requirement was that the recognizable shape of the Absolut bottle appear somewhere in each piece. Pärn was one of many international animators who contributed to the campaign. Pärn's contribution (which, I repeat, was commissioned) shows a man's hand stroking something that swells into the shape of an Absolut bottle. Pärn turned the campaign back on Absolut by criticizing their arrogant display of self-loving. And while those involved deny any censorship, Pärn's contribution was abruptly removed from the Absolut website.

Ironically, *Absolut Pärn* and Czech animator, Michaela Pavlatova's anti-drinking contribution were the best of the commissions.

Priit Pärn,
Time Out, 1984.

Switch off The Lights (winner of a Bronze Lion award at the Cannes International Advertising Festival) is an hilarious energy conservation ad. A man prepares to leave his crying wife and children. Ignoring their cries, he packs his bag, leaves the apartment and heads for the elevator. As he waits for the elevator, he hesitates for a moment. In a flash, he heads back to the apartment. He opens the door: the family turns around, joyfully surprised, only to see that he has returned solely to 'switch off the lights'.

Most recently, Pärn has been working with his former student Ülo Pikkov on a proposed TV series-turned feature film, *Frank and Wendy*. The series is about two paranormal investigators assigned to Estonia to investigate the many strange events that are happening in the strange country.

Pärn also continues to draw caricatures for Estonian as well as foreign magazines and newspapers and his charcoal etchings have been exhibited all over the world.

In 1994, Pärn initiated an animation program at the Turku School of Art and Communication in Finland. The school, which emphasizes the development of ideas over technical training, has met with remarkable international success. In its short existence, the school has already been a three-time Best Animation school nominee at the Ottawa International Student Animation Festival and a number of its individual films have been invited to major international festivals.

Influential as he is, not everyone loves Pärn's work. Some find his films repetitive, sexist, ugly, and illogical ("It is not my problem what some people call my works," Pärn responds.) It is easy to understand some of the criticisms. Because of the accessibility to independent or personal animation, a healthy percentage of the North American animation professionals continue to foolishly believe that Disney animation is the standard, the 'norm', the bible. In that context, Pärn's drawings appear sloppy, fed directly by the Devil. But these are also folks who like their art like they like their food: cheap, simple, and fast. They seek answers not questions.

Pärn's design style has also become so heavily imitated in Estonia and other parts of the world that it is becoming a bit tiresome and Parn's resounding influence on the design styles of many other Estonian animators (Ulo Pikkov, Janno Põldma, Priit Tender, Kasper Jancis) has led a few folks to complain that the apparent complexity in Estonian animation is nothing more than a shell game run by dilettantes. Of course, people often forget that the

Priit Pärn,
Frank and Wendy,
2004.

PÄRN 84

Estonians, with their relatively unique language and roots, often have a different way of processing the world around them.

Easily the biggest charge against Pärn is that his work is sexist. Women, these critics suggest, are little more than superficial, man-abiding creatures who like nothing more than to cook, clean, and fuck. Perhaps these same critics need to take a look at the men in Pärn's films. They are not exactly paragons of wisdom, beauty and truth either. But, hey, I'm a man so I'm probably the wrong person to ask.

One thing is certain: Priit Pärn has fashioned a body of work that, through its very uncertainty, irony and rejection of accessible solutions, succinctly reflects our own complex, absurd and trivial condition. Each of his films asks us to consider how these systems are subtly (and not so subtly) shifting and moulding our actions, thoughts and beliefs. As we become lost in an ever-expanding maze of technology that is turning us away from the outside world, Pärn aspires to show us who we are and where we've come from – while reminding us that it doesn't have to be this way. In so doing, he escapes the constrictions of conventional animation and cartoon storytelling and takes his place as an international citizen in the kingdom of art.

Chapter Eight

Nukufilm: Changing of the Guard

Meanwhile back at Nukufilm ... around 1975, Elbert Tuganov finally realized that he and Pars had aged and that new directors were needed. With the exception of Heins Valk's two attempts in the early 1970s, Tuganov and Pars were the only directors at the studio from 1958–1975. "They were so full of power and energy," says Arvo Nuut, "They didn't lack ideas and did the work that had to be done. But, after that period, they realized that new people were needed." They sought talent that could easily fit into the style and ambitions of the studio.

One of the first to propose a project was Heins Valk, a well-known caricaturist, and later, a politician in Estonia. Valk made two children's films for Nukufilm: *Mis? Kes? Kus?* (What? Who? Where?, 1970) and *Sõbrad* (Friends, 1970). I haven't seen the first film, but *Friends* is a minor film about the relationship between a wolf and a bear, fashioned with cut-out figures.

Well-known Estonian artist Kaarel Kurismaa also made a couple of films at Nukufilm. During the 1970s and 1980s, dada, pop art and kitsch influenced Kurismaa's art. And their traces can be found in both of his puppet films, *Vahva Rätseb* (Master Tailor, 1982) and *Võidusõit* (The Race, 1984). While the bunnies in *Master Tailor* can be deemed 'cute', they engage the mature viewer in such a self-aware manner that it's clear Kurismaa is winking at his adult audience. And his masterful deployment of kitsch, particularly in the forms assumed by the Tailor's yarn-created characters, makes it difficult to distinguish where parody begins and ends.

As with Kalju Kurepõld (whose films have been discussed in Chapter 4), long time Nukufilm animator, Aarne Ahi, was also given the opportunity to make puppet films. Ahi, it seems (I say 'seems' because I was unable to see all of the films by this quartet of directors) was the most successful of the four recruits. His second film, *Linalakk ja Rosalind* (Flaxenhair and Rosalind, 1978) now appears dated. The animation is at times quite poor and the look of the film is quite unimaginative (it was designed by Kurismaa). *Kingikratt* (The House Spirit, 1991), on the other hand, is a well-told and competently animated Christmas tale about a wolf who robs Santa of his presents.

This first group of directors did not meet the studio's hopeful expectations. Part of the problem was that they (Valk, Kurismaa, and Kurepõld) were already mature artists, with already established personal styles. Another problem was they were handed the reigns to a film without any preparatory filmmaking experience. As such, some of the films are simply not very well directed. Perhaps Nukufilm would have had better success if they had followed Rein Raamat's example of using established artists simply as artists first, allowing them to familiarize themselves with the filmmaking apparatus before being given the chance to direct.

After making a few films, everyone but Ahi returned to their prior artistic worlds (although Kurismaa did work as an artist on a number of Nukufilm productions). By the early 1980s, Nukufilm was back to square one. Fortunately, the next stage of the search for animators was more successful because the studio (adopting Rein Raamat's approach) sought young people who had just graduated from post-secondary school and, as such, had not yet matured as artists. This new group included Rao Heidmets, Kalju Kivi, Riho Unt and Hardi Volmer. "They didn't save Estonian puppet animation, but developed it further," says Arvo Nutt. Then again, one could counter-argue that the quartet did in fact save the puppet studio. With Tuganov and Pars clearly running out of steam and with the failure of the previous attempt at securing new directors, Nukufilm was desperately in need of some fresh voices to keep film production going. If these fresh voices did not save Estonian puppet animation, then they certainly preserved it.

Rao Heidmets

Rao Heidmets joined Nukufilm in 1982. He was born in the beautiful Estonian beach town of Parnu. His mother was a teacher and his father was an electrical engineer. "We lived on the outskirts of town in Parnu. Sea, forest and rivers were very close, as was our very small school. It was an old wooden house that was about four minutes from home. If lessons started at 8am, I woke up ten minutes before," recalls Heidmets. Heidmets attended secondary school in Parnu, where future Nukufilm animator Hardi Volmer

was attending along with other future cinéastes like Estonian documentarian, Mark Soosar. During this time, Heidmets developed an interest in cinema and made short 8mm films for fun with classmates.

After secondary school, Heidmets went to Tallinn to study electrical engineering at the Technical University. He had wanted to study biology at Tartu University but acceptance to the program was limited. Heidmets was in a hurry to enrol because within a month he would be called to the Soviet Army: "I started to get afraid and decided to go to Tallinn where there was no competition to study electrical engineering."

Heidmets loathed electrical engineering. "It was hard and too much for me, so during the days I made short 8mm cut-out films with some of my friends." The school also had a film club so Heidmets was able to see a lot of new films, such as *Yellow Submarine*. "This was so new and different to us. You got a taste of what they do elsewhere." Occasionally, Heidmets came across interesting films on Finnish TV and seeing the first films of Priit Pärn were especially memorable: I remember that Pärn's films were so good, interesting and different from Soviet films." Eventually, Heidmets became overwhelmed by his studies and sought escape. "There were always exams and they wanted to throw me out, so I went to the doctor and complained of migraines. I obtained a note saying I could be free from studying for a year."

During that year off in 1979, Heidmets learned that Elbert Tuganov had devised a short animator's course. The studio needed new blood and so they offered a two to three week course where animators demonstrated how puppets move and how animation works in general. Heidmets joined and at the course's end produced a small, yet ultimately impressive, piece: "I made something with a matchbox and they liked it. Tuganov asked me to come to the studio and work as an animator." Heidmets accepted but within the year had to return to his engineering studies. Upon graduation Heidmets had had an agreement to work at Tallinnfilm, but was already obligated to work as an electrician. "I pulled some tricks. I went to the country to do some stupid electrical work. I obtained a work paper stating that the job would entail one month's work. Despite the work order saying I was a carpenter or something, this is what I presented at Tallinnfilm, and I got in."

Heidmets joined Nukufilm in 1982 as an animator and within a year started his first film, *Tuvitädi* (Pigeon Aunt, 1983): "It was a good time for me because they were looking for new talents. I worked with Priit Pärn, my first and only teacher in animation.

He influenced me as a director and a scriptwriter. I managed to watch a lot of films at Tallinnfilm and I especially watched Priit's, observing closely on the cutting table to see how many frames, etc. ... I feel that Priit as a person and a filmmaker is my biggest influence."

Rao Heidmets, *Living Room*, 1993.

Pigeon Aunt is about a big-breasted old woman who tries her best to maintain order outside her apartment complex. A menacing cat, a careless girl, a mischievous boy, and a burglar are constantly thwarting her attempts at peace. Called upon to save the life of the young girl a third time, this time from an oncoming truck, the old woman builds a ramp to re-route the truck. The truck instead strikes the apartment, and destroys it. After the ensuing chaos, the woman puts everything back together. Exhausted, she splits apart and literally becomes a part of the neighbourhood landscapes. Out of harmony comes discord and discord, harmony.

Pigeon Aunt is an innovative film and its use of a three dimensional cut-out technique immediately set it apart from anything previously created at Nukufilm. "I feel that I did what I wanted with *Pigeon Aunt*," says Heidmets, "and remember thinking that the technique was new. The 3D cut-out was Pärn's innovation and I thought that maybe I should adopt this as a style but also thought I should try different things. Maybe this was a mistake. I don't know. But I think each subsequent film I made was different from the last." And perhaps straying from this was an error because Heidmets' next films *Nuril* (1985) *Kaelkirjak* (Giraffe, 1986) and *Serenaad* (Serenade, 1987) were not as successful as *Pigeon Aunt*.

Aside from access to many Soviet films through Tallinnfilm, Heidmets was able to see Western animation when *Giraffe* was invited to the Annecy Animation Festival in 1987. It was an important experience for Heidmets. Not only did Annecy provide the rare chance to travel outside the Soviet Union, but there he realized that Estonian animation was just as good as that of other countries: "We had always heard how bad and technically poor the Soviet films were, so we felt demoralized about our work. In Annecy, I saw that we were at the same level as everyone else."

Heidmet's most successful works are his last three films (excluding the Christmas film, *Päkiapikupuu* (1991)): *Papa Carlo Teater* (Papa Carlo's Theatre, 1988), *Noblesse Oblige* (1989), and *Elutuba* (Living Room, 1994).

Papa Carlo, made in collaboration with Priit Pärn, uses the puppet theatre as an allegory for a desensitized world where atrocities and violence are an everyday reality. In the film, a series of puppet theatre performances are staged. Each puppet is attached to a set of strings controlled by another large puppet positioned above. A

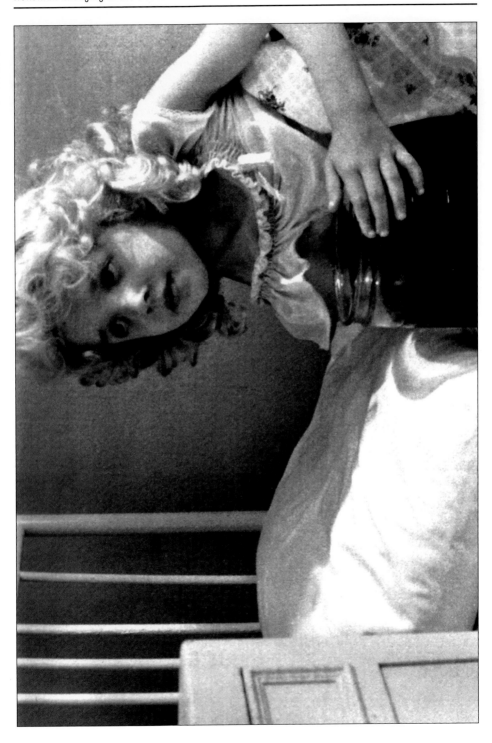

woman performs acrobatic stunts on a bike; a magician does a box-cutting trick. All the while violent images of sliced and burning boxes occur in the background. After each performance, the master puppeteer tosses the puppet away. In the end, a pianist puppet breaks free of the puppeteer and a calm prevails. The progressively aggressive, fast-paced music of the film's score is replaced by a quiet piano piece and, for the first time, we see the doors of the theatre open. And beyond the doors, we see the puppets scattered like corpses. Freedom has its price.

Heidmets' use of human-sized puppets in *Papa Carlo* is visually unique for animation, let alone Estonian animation. Complementing the displays of the grotesque puppets is Olav Ehala's frenetic score, complete with a violent and ugly guitar solo. The music's disruptive nature coupled with the rapid editing creates an atmosphere of tension, fear, and chaos – a world where no one knows what awaits.

Despite *Papa Carlo's* success (it was selected for screening at Cannes), Heidmets remains unsatisfied with the film. "*Papa Carlo* reflects the historical period when we were fighting for freedom and it is very political. I never thought of making political films but I guess the era affected me. I find *Papa Carlo* too political and too dark."

In *Noblesse Oblige,* Heidmets, again using large puppets, turns his attention to the family. A bourgeois family arrives for dinner at the house of some materially proficient friends. As they await dinner, the characters lounge awkwardly about the house, with nothing to do or say. The artificial features and staccato movements of the puppets serve to lampoon the bland superficiality of these people. An attempt to inject some life into the dinner party by a violin-playing boy is violently rebutted. To reinforce the banality of this family, Heidmets cleverly repeats actions and sounds throughout the film. He also toys with movement and perception as the figures shift back and forth from human actors to puppets. Heidmets' use of life- size puppets adds an additional element of realism and, alternately of the grotesque to his dark critique of the wastefulness and stagnancy of this class.

Elutuba is Heidmets' most successfully realised film, mixing scratch animation and pixilation. *Elutuba* examines the generational relationship between a woman, her father, and her young daughter. The old man is lost in a world hampered by mortality and strict definitions. Anything that questions his standards is literally scratched out of the picture. The young girl's world is one of discovery, wherein tadpoles, dolls, weddings and plants awaken her to life. Meanwhile, her mother is preoccupied by a world of desire. Eventually the girl tires of being neglected and unloved. She too begins to scratch the images to gain control of her world and embrace her mother and grandfather within it. The final image of the girl's scribbled drawing of a playground in which the trio is united is both poignant and powerful. Heidmets' use of high contrast film, along with the violence of the scratched images and their stuttering pixilated movements, all combine to create the film's dark, tentative and tense tone.

After completing *Elutuba*, Heidmets turned away from animation to make a feature film for children, *Kallis Härra Q* (Dear Mr. Moon, 1998), a live-action short, *Heinaloom* (The Grass Bird, 2001), and to head the Children and Youth program at Estonian State TV from 1999–2001. In 2003 he returned to animation and made, *Instinct*. In this light critique of cloning, a creator loses control over his creations and all hell breaks loose. Heidmets recently completed *Pärlimees* (The Pearlman, 2005), a visually innovative film about the diffcultly a nation faces maintaining and protecting their indigenous culture from outside forces.

Heidmets is quite humble and matter-of-fact about his work. "I don't feel that I must say something to the world or that my films are so great that people must hear them," says Heidmets. "It's not so pressing for me to do things. I enjoy the process of making a film. I like the six-month brain workout ... when you must always be thinking. You never know what the results will be because you make changes all the time. I like to draw and every time I begin with the thought that I just want to draw a nice naked woman. I draw and draw and, in the end, I still create the picture I envisioned. That's why I try again and again. Maybe I'll stop after I find my perfect film and move on to something else."

Kalju Kivi

In terms of quality and diversity of techniques, Kalju Kivi is the most ambitious and exciting animator in Estonia. Since his first film, *Paperileht* (Sheet of Paper, 1981), Kivi has animated with objects, puppets, photo collage, cut-out, string, fabric, and pixilation. The results have not always been successful, but they are always interesting.

Kivi was born in Tartu. His father was a draftsman and his mother was a teacher. Because their Tartu apartment was so small and cramped, Kivi spent much of his time with his grandparents in Otepää. "My grandfather and grandmother lived in their own house and had a large yard," says Kivi, "I saw the first film of my life in Otepää – *Oliver Twist*. I was rather little at the time and the chase scenes in the slums of London haunted my dreams for some

Kalju Kivi. time. Years later, when I saw the film again, I found out where my nightmares came from."

While studying at the Estonian State Art Institute, Kivi worked on the popular Estonian television show for children, *Saturday Evening with Father*. It was here that Elbert Tuganov spotted Kivi and asked him if he'd like to give animation a try. "This was such an unexpected and, at the same time, tempting challenge. I did not hesitate," recalls Kivi, "I saw it as my opportunity for a kind of self-realisation. As fate would have it, I was among a group of students at the Art Institute that had experimented some in film and had tried a little bit of animation."

Because of the shortage of directors at Nukufilm, Kivi was given the opportunity to direct a film almost immediately. Kivi found his new environment both spirited and supportive. "I was full of energy and did not pay much attention to the advice others offered me. I had a pretty clear idea of the story I wanted to tell. The attitude toward me at Nukufilm was very favourable and that just added to my eagerness. I grasped the systematic nature of animation pretty quickly and consequently wanted to attempt something new with each subsequent film. I tried to use different kinds of materials or tried changing the style of motion. I did not have any teachers as such. Everyone gave me a hint here or a pointer there and that helped me move forward."

The conflict of the individual within larger institutional barriers is at the core of much of Kivi's work. *Sheet of Paper*, *Sõlm*, (Knot, 1983), *Miks Puud Ei Kõnele? (Why don't the Trees Speak?*, 1988), *Sokk* (Goat, 1991) *Humachinoid* (1995) examine conflicts between individuals and the state. In *Sheet of Paper* – which shows the influence of Heino Pars' *Nail* through its anthropomorphic treatment of various office supplies – a sheet of paper breaks free from a pack of papers but then must confront a variety of menacing obstacles (glue, ink, scissors, stapler etc. …) in its bid for freedom. The parallel to Soviet society is obvious yet Kivi's theme is universal: an individual's on-going search for one's own rhythm, within any society, involves the overcoming of many obstacles.

In *Knot*, we first see two loose bits of blue and red string. Then, the creator's hand enters the frame to tie the two strings together. The strings evolve into two characters. With echoes of Norman McLaren's *Neighbours*, the 'men' busy themselves by trying to figure out how to get rid of this knot that binds them. Sometimes they cooperate, at other times they fight. After successive failures in ridding themselves of the knot, the creator's hand returns to move the knot so that the two men become one. We're all in this shit together … man. Philosophy aside, *Knot* is well animated and the continual metamorphosis of the 'men' into various shapes and forms is smoothly executed, especially for an artist only making his second animation film.

Why don't The Trees Speak? is a powerful and unique film in the Estonian canon. A man (played by Kivi) enters a forest and slowly begins cutting down trees. An initially serene and almost spiritual undertaking soon turns into a feverish and murderous assault as the man runs about madly and frantically cutting down every tree in his way. The film is pixilated and shot in black and white. The film's jittery time-lapse pace accentuates the alternation between the long and close shots, giving the film a schizophrenic quality. The forest is friendly and inviting one moment and ominous the next as the trees menacingly tower over the man. In a final act of madness, the man 'executes' a gigantic tree. Its death is shown from a variety of perspectives. The man collapses to the ground exhausted.

Goat, the most playful of Kivi's works, is an abstract expressionist piece for kids about a goat that sees his reflection in water. When the goat's reflected image begins in turn to look strangely at the 'real' goat, all certainty about reality and illusion go out the window. From there, the goat's reflection shatters into many more, while colourful shapes and forms dance on the screen. You can certainly apply egghead logic here and uncover the theme of self-awareness and its construction of identity, but *Goat* is also just a really swell and colourful film for kids to giggle at.

Humachinoid, made a few years after Estonian independence, examines the role of the individual within changing political systems. A man walks against a background of always changing collage images. He dutifully and robotically wears either the attire of a soldier or that of a businessman and marches along to a tune whose origin is in some unknown elsewhere. Kivi suggests, rather cynically, that a change in political systems will not really change the individual's status as a mere cog.

Bride of Star and *Kaleidoscope* are perhaps Kivi's strongest works. *Bride of Star* is based on an Estonian folk song and tells the story of a girl wooed by both the moon and the sun. In the end she accepts neither – as the title tell us. The most intriguing aspects of the film are its narration, which is all sung, and the incredible backgrounds and designs that are fashioned from rope and fabric. "In the Soviet era," adds Kivi, "the use of this kind of intensely nationalist form and subject demonstrated that one belonged to this particular people and culture. It was also a protest of sorts against propaganda and mass culture that were obtruding. I think this is one subject that can still captivate me."

Kalju Kivi,
Humachinoid, 1995.

Kaleidscope's raw materials are coloured shards of glass, used to document the evolution of the planet. From the random motion of objects begins a transformation, resulting in more stable, predictable and recognizable natural and human shapes. "It was pure joy to play with colours and see the emergence of a kind of story through this game," adds Kivi, "The unorthodox work process was such that Erki-Sven Tüür composed music based solely on the film script. Then I filmed the entire story with an animation rostrum camera and the shards of glass, with the music acting as the inspiration."

Since independence, Kivi has spent most of his time working with the Estonian National Puppet Theatre, primarily as a set designer: "The offer from the Puppet Theatre was unexpected and I did not hesitate for a moment at the proposition. By that time, the opportunities offered to me by puppet film had been exhausted and I had also taken my first steps as an art director for live-action feature films."

Kivi's career shift was also motivated by Estonian independence and its effect on animation production. "One's responsibility in making a film is greater today. You have to generate sure-fire ideas and the opportunities for experimentation and risk taking have decreased." Kivi did begin a film called *Eilne Vedur* (Yesterday's Engine), but his other interests forced him to abandon the project to younger colleague Mikk Rand who completed the film in 2000. Since then, Kivi has abandoned animation work altogether.

Riho Unt and Hardi Volmer.

In appraising his own work, Kivi remains unsatisfied in some respects yet generally pleased with what he was able to achieve: "It was exciting for me to bring different materials to life and watch the way they played. That was what fascinated me. I have not consciously sought my own style or character, but my stories are probably all a little bit similar. In other words, I have tried to tell one story in different ways and through different materials."

The Brothers: Riho Unt and Hardi Volmer

As I was walking down a hallway at Eesti Film Archives, I noticed an old (circa 1980s) photo of two shabbily dressed guys toasting each other. They looked like mirror reflections of one another: similar suit, beard, and glasses. The two men in the picture are Riho Unt and Hardi Volmer. Not surprisingly, the similarities between the two extend beyond their looks; they were school friends and artistic partners on a number of animation films. They were so close that they were often referred to as 'brothers.'

Riho Unt was born in 1956 in Harku-Risti, a small county just outside of Tallinn. "I consider myself Estonian," says Unt, "although it's said that my grandparents are Germans. There's a rumour that something may have happened between my grandmother and the landlord."

Both of Unt's parents were involved with agriculture. His father was a veterinary surgeon and his mother dealt with cattle. Unt's father was adept at drawing and it stimulated his son to give it a try. Unt initially wanted to study architecture after high school, but "unfortunately mathematics were a weak point." Instead he chose interior design, "where you didn't need math so much." At the Tallinn Academy, Unt met up with Kalju Kivi and Hardi Volmer. The trio made amateur 16mm live-action films, including one silly, but pretty funny film called *Charlie Goes To Tallinn*. "We were just fooling around, but excerpts of the films were shown on Estonian Television and were terribly popular," says Unt. The films were made under the banner, Paratrust, a term whose English translation would approximate "backside" or "rear-end" or "ass." Paratrust was a sort of underground performance group that made films and performed music.

Unt's entrance into animation, like many Estonian animators, was

quite by chance. After graduating from Interior Design, Unt was offered a job at a furniture factory in Narva. "I didn't think it was a good idea to take the job as there were no good materials available for furniture making at the time."

Meanwhile, Kivi was already at Nukufilm and told Unt of a vacancy at the studio. Unt came on board as an animator on Kivi's film, *Sõlm* (Noose, 1983). "I didn't enjoy the experience," says Unt, "I was an interior designer forced to work as an animator." Nevertheless, Unt persevered and within a year was making his first animation film.

The other 'brother', Hardi Volmer, was born in Parnu. Both his parents were designers. They did advertising for shop windows as well as interior design. Volmer's father also had an interest in animation. "There was a short time when my father was interested in 8mm film," recalls Volmer, "He made flat animation fairy tales as a hobby. They were really interesting. He was interested in movement and how to animate. When I saw how it worked, I too became interested."

When Volmer was a teenager he started making films, including a puppet film, with friends. His exposure to different types of animation was somewhat limited: "We saw mostly Soviet animation or typical Disney-style stuff. I don't remember seeing anything that exciting or experimental, Finnish TV did provide an outlet. *Yellow Submarine* played in cinemas and when I was maybe in 6th or 7th grade and studied in Parnu a group of us boys skipped school and bought a bus ticket to Tallinn to see *Yellow Submarine*."

After secondary school, Volmer went to Tallinn to study interior design (where he met Riho Unt), but then switched over to stage design. During his studies, Volmer continued to toy around with film. "The school had a 16mm camera and we made gag films." Volmer was also a part of Partrust, whose members also included Rao Heidmets (whom Unt and Volmer met through a mutual friend).

Volmer came to animation through Unt. "Riho suggested that we make a film together," says Volmer. The timing was good for us. The old Nukufilm gang was tired and preparing to go and there was a hole that needed to be filled with new young filmmakers. Otherwise, it would have been more complicated to become a director immediately at the studio. You usually had to work toward this position step by step." "They sort of trusted us," says Unt, "and trust was a very dubious thing in those days, but they knew Hardi and I had previously worked together and they let us make a film."

Their first film, *Imeline näär)iöö* (Wonderful New Year's Eve,

1984), is based on a story by Estonian writer Hando Runnel. They set out to make a nice Christmas story, even though Christmas was unmentionable under the Soviet time. To circumvent this little irony, they titled the film with an older Estonian word that translated as New Year instead of Christmas.

The film begins in the back room of a shop where two unsold toys – a doll and a toy swan – embark on a quest to find the family that snubbed them. In the end, upon finding the family, the doll and the swan turn 'real'. Besides its undeniable charm, the strength of the film resides, not surprisingly, in its set design. The recreation of Parnu's old wooden homes is remarkably detailed and accurate and the camerawork, especially in the opening scene, is as graceful as a dancer.

While the film was well-received and won a Diploma for Best Debut film at the All-Union Film festival, it encounter the usual bizarre censorship issues. "We had funny problems," says Volmer, "because censors found some scenes too sexy for children. Originally, the doll that turns into a living child comes cheek to cheek with another child. It was nothing ... but some felt it was too sexy." In the re-tooled version, a sexless embrace replaces the cheek smooch.

Most importantly, *Wonderful New Year's Eve* showed that Volmer and Unt worked well as a team. "We were both designers, directors and script writers but it worked," says Volmer, "We are very similar but we also fill each other's gaps."

"We were in sync," adds Unt, "and it was comfortable to work together. Every film started from an idea. We'd sit together, create a storyboard together and then decide what each of us would do: It would not have made sense to duplicate everything but we shared the basic responsibilities."

Like in the early days, Nukufilm was full of fresh new faces and, as such, there was a lot of positive energy at the studio. "The studio was out of the city almost in a forest," says Volmer, "and everyday we rode a special Tallinnfilm bus to the countryside. There was nothing but nature around. The whole team was really close and it was a lovely feeling to work in such an environment."

For their next film, *Nõiutud saar* (Enchanted Island, 1985) the 'brothers' went beyond Estonian borders for their source material. "We were reading these North Siberian/Iberian fairytales. The stories were very crazy and non-linear. We were familiar with concrete fairytales but here we saw something different," says Volmer, " The central element of the film was to be the design. Unt had been experimenting with unconventional forms while at school and drew upon past inspiration for the characters of the film. The tribal characters of the film have small heads and their arms and legs expand and compress like an accordion. They can also turn their legs into shells of boats, their arms into paddles or transform into flying machines.

As the tribe goes about its daily routine of fishing and dancing, one member sees a gigantic, menacing whale swallow, and then release, the island. No one appears to have seen the incident, nor is it clear whether it's been entirely dreamed up by this one tribe member. While the rest continue to dance, the 'man' turns himself into a flying machine and ventures up to the clouds where he encounters a variety of strange characters with shape-shifting abilities. In the end, the man defeats the whale and returns to his tribe, who remained unaware of his battles. Was it real? A dream? A bad mushroom trip?

Accepted at the Annecy Festival in France, *Enchanted Island* was Unt/Volmer's first film shown in the West. "Riho and I had never even been abroad, not even to Finland," says Volmer, "It was very exciting to have the opportunity to see these films and there were so many. I think this was when we saw *Street of Crocodiles* [by The Brothers Quay] and afterwards we thought, 'oh, what shit we are doing at home.'"

For their next film, *Kevadine Kärbes* (Spring Fly, 1986), they returned to an Estonian source, the famous writer A.M. Taamsare. A mosquito and a fly meet to engage in a philosophical dialogue about free will and determinism.

Next came *Sõda* (The War, 1988), which is, in many ways, a very simple film. A small bat occupies an abandoned factory. He goes about his life in peace, disturbing no one. One day, rats arrive and overtake the building, thereby disrupting the bat's life. Later, crows arrive and do the same. Finally, the rats and the crows fight each other and, in turn, destroy the bat's home. The parallel to the German-Russian occupation of Estonia during the early 1940s is obvious, but the strength of *The War* derives from the universality of its warning. This has happened and could still – anywhere.

"We wanted to make a film in a natural environment," says Volmer, "something very old, rustic, some kind of ruin or country house. We went on a boat trip to Southern Estonia and where there were a lot of old water mills. Later we drove around outside of Tallinn to find similar places. Then we started to create the story from the environment. What could happen in such a place? War, probably." They briefly considered using human-sized puppets but, as Rao Heidmets was making *Papa Carlo*, they didn't want to copy him.

Sõda (The War) was the 'brothers' fourth collaboration together

Riho Unt, Hardi Volmer, A Miraculous Christmas Night, 1984.

Riho Unt, Hardi Volmer, Enchanted Island, 1985.

and while they 'reunited' to make two more films (*Twilight Romance* and *Primavera*), neither is up to the standard of their quartet of earlier works. "It was a natural development," says Unt, "At a certain moment we developed in different ways. Later we tried to work together a couple of times but the films are not as good as the earlier ones. At the beginning of our collaboration we were beginners in animation, so the interest to create something new kept us together."

"When making our first few films we did everything together," says Volmer, "Everything was discussed between us. But as time went on, differences started to creep in. From then on, it wasn't so easy."

Since independence, Unt has been more the more successful of the two in animation. Volmer is a multi-takser who has worked in animation, theatre and cinema. While Volmer has had success with feature films like *All My Lenins*, his animation films, for the most part, have been disappointing. Solo animation shorts, *Works and Doings, Something Else, Incipit Vita Nova, and Barbarians* are interesting but are hindered by technical and conceptual weaknesses.

Meanwhile, Unt spent the 1990s preoccupied with his 'Samuel' Trilogy: *Kapsapea* (Cabbagehead, 1993), *Kapsapea 2: Tagasi Euroopasse* (Cabbagehead 2: Back to Europe, 1997) and *Sammueli Internet* (Samuel's Internet, 2000)

Cabbagehead is based on a popular turn-of-the-century Estonian play written by Oskar Lutso. Updated for contemporary audiences (and influenced by the films *Raiders of The Lost Ark* and *It's a Mad Mad Mad Mad World*), *Cabbagehead* focuses on Samuel, a stubborn farmer who steals his neighbour's gigantic cabbage in the hopes of winning the top prize (five roubles) at the state fair. Word of Samuel's impressive cabbage spreads and soon everyone wants a piece of it. Samuel, aided by Harrison (yes ... as in Harrison Ford, aka Indiana Jones), the New York Times reporter who broke the story, flees from a variety of clownish figures: Soviet and Chinese military officials, a masked burglar, and a New York taxi driver. In the end, Samuel does escape, but the cabbage blows up, literally, in his face. Samuel is left with nothing.

While *Cabbagehead* clearly addresses issues of Estonian independence (i.e. everyone will want a piece of Estonia), the film's obvious commercial ambitions are of more interest. Unt admits that artistic factors were secondary: "We were consciously trying to make something more commercial." Unfortunately, Unt had not seen any of the stop-motion films from England's Aardman Animation (the creators of *Wallace and Gromit* and *Chicken Run*).

Riho Unt, Hardi Volmer, *Springfly*, 1986.

Riho Unt, Hardi Volmer, *The War*, 1987.

Cabbagehead, despite a strong script and animation, is a decidedly primitive film that pales in comparison to the smooth, professional look of Aardman's work.

Riho Unt, *Back to Europe*, 1997.

More importantly, *Cabbagehead* suggested a new reality for Estonian animation: a commercial marketplace. "You have to think more of the audience these days and you have to work harder and be more precise about what you are doing," says Unt, "During Soviet times, you could pour all of your stress and problems into your metaphoric work. These days, you can't do that anymore. The financial side requires different thinking. In those days, you didn't have to worry about where the money was coming from. These days your story has to be good and well thought out." Clearly, *Cabbagehead* signalled a new era for Estonian animators.

The two entertaining but uneven sequels, *Back To Europe* and *Samuel's Internet*, follow the model established with *Cabbagehead*: light political criticism mixed with high adventure and a comic narrative. In *Back to Europe*, a not-so-subtle critique of Estonia's desire to join the European Union, an impoverished Samuel discovers oil, only to have it stolen by a trio of European Union thugs. The new Union it seems isn't really that different from the old Union. In *Samuel's Internet (2000)*, Samuel and his pet pig literally get sucked into the Internet where they meet a variety of popular game characters as well as pornography models and cause havoc for the controllers of the Internet: the Pentagon. It is by far the weakest of Unt's trilogy. And it's never quite clear throughout the series whether Samuel is meant to take the piss out of Estonian peasant yokels or if Unt shares Samuel's occasionally reactionary views.

Hing Sees (Having Soul, 2002) is taken from an A.H. Taamsare story about a young boy who wishes his toy soldiers would have souls so that they may close their eyes when shot. "I had intended it to be a nice Christmas story for children," says Unt, "but there was a change of cameraman and animators so I couldn't get the result I wanted. So the story became simpler and out of a nice story, it eventually became a horror story." And the film almost succeeds. The character design is interesting, bold and expressive and the story is powerful, but Unt has trouble sustaining the tension and almost chilling atmosphere of the film. As a result, it feels like a long 18 minutes.

Unt's most recent film, *Vennad karusüdamed* (Brothers Bearhearts, 2005) is a story about the adventures of three bear cubs from the painting, *Morning in the Pine Forest*, by Russian artist, Ivan Shiskin. Upon completing a painting of the three bear cubs playing in the forest, the mother bear is killed by a hunter. The

Riho Unt, *Having Soul*, 1985.

hunter discovers the painting, likes it, and signs his name on it. Five years pass and the bear cubs (Henry, Vincent, and August) are now struggling artists living in Paris. Their attempts to sell their art meet with repeated failure. The Parisian galleries only want realist art like Shiskin's paintings. When the cubs discover that Shishkin has taken credit for their mother's painting, they decide to return to Moscow to hunt down the murderer.

With its beautiful sets and backgrounds (all inspired by modern paintings), and engaging storyline, *Brother's Bearheart* is Unt's most complete and inspired film to date. Using the guise of an adventure story, Unt is really telling us the story of the troubled origins of modern art – both past and present.

Nukufilm's choice of Heidmets, Kivi, Unt and Volmer has been a fortuitous one. All four are heavily involved in a variety of artistic and cultural fields in Estonia today and have all had international success with their films. Certainly it appears to have been harder over at Nukufilm than at Joonisfilm. Unt is the only one who remains consistently visible at Nukufilm. With limited funding, there are few opportunities to make films. Volmer has been busy in theatre; Heidmets with live-action films and television production; and Kivi with puppet theatre work.

The fragmentation of Nukufilm has hurt the studio to some degree. But, on the other hand, the scattered nature of the studio has ensured that a wide array of voices have been given the chance to be heard. The happy result: Nukufilm has no single aesthetic style – like the Priit Pärn 'style' that Joonisfilm might be said to possess.

Riho Unt is the creative backbone of Nukufilm. He is an incredibly focussed and generous artist. When he's not working on his own films, he's actively tutoring a number of young, aspiring animation artists just as Tuganov and Pars did before him (perhaps not as directly). By sharing his personal experience and knowledge as well as that acquired in part through Tuganov and Pars, Unt is like a bridge linking the young animators with the 'grandfathers'. And yet during this process, he has also been acquiring new ways of thinking and seeing from his younger colleagues. Nukufilm is a fine example of how the oral tradition within Estonian animation has maintained an active dialogue between past and present.

Chapter Nine

Music, Please

Music is such an integral part of Estonian animation and Estonian culture in general, that it certainly warrants a brief chapter of its own to introduce some of the most important music contributors.

While there are many famous animation film composers (e.g. Canada's Normand Roger who has scored numerous animation films including the Oscar winners *The Old Man and The Sea* and *Father and Daughter)*, they remain largely unknown outside of that particular community. In Estonia, it is an entirely different scenario. Some of the prominent musicians who've also worked in animation – Boris Kõrver, Arvo Pärt, Lepo Sumera, Olav Ehala and Sven Grünberg are also well known (especially Pärt) outside of the animation and film worlds. Boris Kõrver, one of the first composers to lend his talents to animation, and specifically to *Little Peter's Dream*, was a well-known composer at the time in Estonia. "We were small fry," says Elbert Tuganov, "and what we said carried no weight. But when Kõrver asked for something or made a suggestion, it meant something since he had all those honorary ranks. He was our guardian angel and he made our first five films."

It was expected in the Soviet days that each animated film would have its own composer (documentary film, for example, was not given money for original music). The State had money set aside for this purpose. Having a little extra money enabled the animators to lure Estonian composers like Kõrver and most notably, Arvo Pärt, who was a relatively unknown composer in Estonia during the 1960s.

Tuganov was always looking around to see who was out there and he had heard some of Pärt's pieces, liked them and invited him to score some films. "[Pärt] was a young man at the time and it was a good source of extra money for him," says Tuganov, "He was not very healthy. He tended to fall ill and he had to be very careful about what he ate. He was happy working with us; he was a more cheerful person back then. There was another man named Lille,

the husband of Finnish estophile Eva Lille, who was a contempo-   Lepo Sumera.
rary of Pärt's. They worked together. When Pärt composed, Lille
played his music for us."

Pärt scored a number of films for both Heino Pars and Elbert
Tuganov from 1961–1974. Pärt's more pop-inspired animation
scores will shock those familiar only with his later famous
"tintinnabuli" style. The groovy organ-driven sounds in *Kõps on
the Uninhabited Island* showcases Pärt's awareness of what we now
deem lounge or elevator music, And the sped up rock and roll
soundtrack of *Mousehunt* shows that Pärt did once have a sense
of humour.

Perhaps the most interesting of Pärt's scores are his contributions
to Tuganov's films *Atomic Boy* and *Atomic Boy and The Warlord*.
In these films, Pärt uses a variety of instruments, including what
sounds like a xylophone, and a variety of percussive and industrial
sounds. The high-pitch piano notes are reminiscent of Norman
McLaren's handmade sounds on his classic film, *Neighbours*.

And best of all, Pärt shows that he was a fine cheese maker too.
Imagine if Erik Satie had written his *Gymnopédies* after coming
home from the shopping mall with hundreds of pretty handker-
chiefs, then proceeding to celebrate his joy by speeding up his
famous trilogy and complementing it with a vocal track by an
adult trying to impersonate a whiny, screeching, tinny-sounding
child. If you close your eyes now and imagine those horrifying
sounds, you've got an inkling of what the cloying main theme of
Atomic entails.

Seriously though, Pärt's contributions are unique, playful, intelligent and interesting. They uncover the lighter side of this sombre
and serious artist, while showing his familiarity with a wide range
of musical styles. It's a shame that he no longer scores animation
because it would certainly be interesting to see how he might have
worked with the Surrealism influenced Estonian animators.

Lepo Sumera

Lepo Sumera was just 50 years old when his life was cut short in
2000. But in those short years he distinguished himself as one of
Estonia's key composers, while serving as a link between older
composers like Heino Jürisalu (who also composed scores for
Elbert Tuganov) and younger composers like Erkki Sven-Tüür
(who was a Sumera student).

After studying under Estonian music pioneer Heino Eller, Sumera
worked as a recording manager at Estonian radio, taught at the
Estonian Music Academy in 1978 and served as the chairman of
the Estonian Composer's Association from 1993 until his death.

Sumera, a popular figure in Estonia, also held the position of   Sven Grünberg.
Minister of Culture from 1988–1992. His musical style was an
amalgam of the traditional Estonian runic song and modern
electronic music. In fact, he was the first Estonian musician to
compose on a computer.

Sumera composed scores for about seventy films, many of which
were animation films. Sumera contributed scores to a number of
Rein Raamat films, most notably *Hell*. In *Hell*, Sumera commu-
nicates the schizophrenia of modern humanity through two
memorable pieces of music: a sensitive, seductive tango and an
explosively exhilarating Nino Rota-inspired circus music meets
can-can score. The can-can piece in particular, with its increasingly
frenetic pace, perfectly captures that point between unharnessed
joy and volatile madness.

Sumera also contributed scores to the first four of Riho Unt and
Hardi Volmer's films. *Springfly*, with its seductive and hypnotic
accordion-led waltz, and *The War*, with a more ambitious orches-
tral score featuring heavy percussion, stand out as fine examples
of how a composer, especially in a medium like animation, where
every sound must be created from scratch, can elevate the overall
film to a new level of power and drama.

The Dynamic Duo: Olav Ehala and Sven Grünberg

Most of the contemporary Nukufilm and Joonisfilm animation
film scores were composed by either Olav Ehala or Sven Grünberg
have composed most of the contemporary Nukufilm and Joonisfilm animation film scores. Ehala's renown stems mostly from his
contributions to Priit Pärn's films (*Breakfast in The Grass*, *Hotel E*,
1895, *The Night of The Carrots*), while Grünberg has contributed
scores to Janno Põldma's *Birthday* and *On The Possibility of Love*
and Ülo Pikkov's *Bermuda* and *The Headless Horseman*, among
others.

Sven Grünberg

Grünberg's initiation into film composition began with Aarne
Ahi's *Liigub? Liigub!* (Moving? Moving!, 1977). Prior to that, he
was very active in rock music as a singer, organist and piano player.
In 1974, he established Mess, the first progressive rock group in
the Soviet Union.

"Our family was very musical," says Grünberg, "My father played
jazz piano for most of his life, but also bass, accordion, trumpet
and organ." Grünberg first touched an electronic instrument (his
father's band organ) in 1964. "My mother liked to sing; my sister
played classical piano and, for some years, was a well-known pop

singer." Beyond the musical education he received at home, Grünberg formalized his training by studying music theory at the Tallinn Music College.

Since 1977, Grünberg has worked on a number of films including features, documentaries and animation films. As Grunberg has written in the notes to a recent 3-disc collection of film music, he relishes the challenge that film brings: "As a rule, the composer is the sole author of a creative work. However, in a movie the musician has, to put it mildly, to consider others, to be just part of a larger whole that synthesizes different fields of art. This requires overcoming one's own ego; for many, this can turn out to be an obstacle beyond his strength."

Composing for film has also forced Grünberg to work at an unaccustomed, quick pace: "In movie production, making the music is the last creative stage, so movie making has taught me to act fast; too often I've had to be in the role of a fire extinguisher. After all deadlines have been hopelessly passed, desperate eyes turn to the composer, who is expected to do big things with a speed faster than sound. I am generally the type who absorbs into a piece, deep and for long."

But the challenge of composing for live-action films pales in comparison to that of animation. "Unlike live-action film, there are no natural sounds at all in animation," says Grünberg, "You must create the entire sound field. This gives style to the film and a more important role to the music."

Despite working with a wide array of animators (Avo Paistik, Janno Põldma, Ülo Pikkov), Grünberg finds little difference between them. "It's maybe strange, but basically they all work in quite similar ways. Ülo Pikkov is younger so I'm also his teacher. I think my experience in this field is beneficial to him. The animators all are very creative and we listen to each other. It's important. Although I'm involved from the beginning, it's better not to be near all the time. Because, in the end, I must write music to the final cut."

"Sven Grünberg's music is quite inspirational to me and half of my films are his music," says Janno Põldma, "He has taught me a lot about how to understand and use music in film." Knowing that Grünberg had collaborated with Avo Paistik, Põldma asked Grünberg to score his first film, *Brothers and Sisters* (1991). "I wasn't sure he would do it, but he said, 'why not?' Tallinnfilm rented the Linnahall (a big concert hall in Tallinn) for twenty-four hours and we spent the whole time making the music," recalls Põldma.

Põldma works with Grünberg from the very beginning of the

film's pre-production. "First, we speak about the film. Then Sven plays short pieces for me and waits for my opinion. I deliberate; is it the right music for the film? If it is, Sven keeps working. If not, he starts again," says Põldma. In particular, Põldma admires Grünberg's team player attitude. "He listens to a director's remarks. He knows that a composer's not the most important role and that it's essential that the director and the composer work as a team."

Grünberg does not simply view himself as a composer making music; he tries to create the entire sound field. "Sven listens to all backgrounds as part of the music," adds Põldma, "Quite often this creates problems between him and the sound engineer. And then I must step in like a teacher to break up the two naughty boys." Because Grünberg focuses on the entire background of a film, he says earlier Estonian film composers have not influenced him: "I'm trying to create the entire sound field while they are only worried about the music. That's the difference."

And despite the decreasing funds available for film musicians, Grünberg relishes the opportunity to take more control of all aspects of the music. "It's better in this way because one person creates the entire sound field in one style." And with technology, Grünberg is now able to spend less time recording and more time composing not only music, but sound.

Olav Ehala

"If we go back to childhood," says Ehala, "I remember seeing puppet films like *Little Scooter* and *Little Peter's Dream*. I was deeply impressed by the films and Arvo Pärt's music and thought it would be nice to make something like that myself." By 1974, that hope came true. During his studies at the Tallinn Conservatory, Ehala was commissioned to do his first film score. A short time later, a mutual friend introduced him to Priit Pärn and, as Pärn needed music for *And Plays Tricks*, so began their ongoing collaboration. "Priit wanted something different," recalls Ehala, "And as our views of life and sense of humour were similar I made music for this particular film and every Pärn film since." Thanks to Pärn, Ehala has also scored music for virtually every other Estonian animator (notably Rao Heidmets, Riho Unt, and Heiki Ernits).

While most composers begin with short films before graduating to features, not so with Ehala. And of the differences between the feature and the animation short, Ehala says: "With live-action I have more time to develop a musical theme. In animation there is very little time. You have maybe twenty seconds compared to

Olav Ehala. three minutes so it requires a different degree of work. Sometimes I have the basic music and then adjust it to the motion so sometimes I would say that animation requires more work than live- action films."

Financial limitations, especially since independence, have provided another stumbling block for the contemporary film composer. Whereas Raamat, Tuganov, and Pars, for example, could employ full orchestras at times, this is simply not feasible today. As such, Ehala has the additional challenge of trying to re-create the sound of an orchestra by himself: "The score is played by myself – with the help of electronics. If you don't listen too carefully you can hear a live orchestra."

Ehala did get an opportunity to use live players for Pärn's *Exercise for An Independent Life*. "All the music was played by live musicians in the cinema studio. We started during the afternoon and finished the next morning. This would be impossible today," says Ehala. Nevertheless, Ehala feels that while you cannot replace a single player, you can replace a big orchestra. And there are those who are surprised to learn that certain scores (e.g. *Hotel E*) were electronically created.

Pärn and Ehala work together almost from the first seeds of the film's original idea. "It's quite difficult to explain the process," says Ehala, "because sometimes Priit shows me images without any animation or sometimes we meet at the editing table and look through episodes."

"Knowing that music is a weak point for me," says Pärn, "I try to deal with it from the earliest stages because both audio and visual are equally important." Once Pärn finishes a storyboard, he begins to have a clearer sense of what music is required. "I don't know what the music should be exactly, but I know what I want at a certain place. It's very intuitive." For the first part of *Breakfast on The Grass*, Pärn wanted old Estonian work songs. In *Time Out*, he wanted a reggae beat to convey the feeling of one thing growing out of another. With *Hotel E*, Ehala and Pärn had the idea of using repetition, of introducing a theme that didn't go anywhere. Pärn suggested using a bit from *Ode to Joy*. Ehala then composed something similar to create a feeling of stagnation and underline the film's political point about changing political systems only being superficially different.

The working relationship between the two men is so balanced that there have been occasions when not only has a Pärn sequence led Ehala to alter his music, but the reverse too. With *Exercises for an Independent Life*, Pärn actually found the ending of the film by listening to the music at the beginning, thereby changing the roles of the little boy and the man.

The smooth and intimate nature of their working relationship further extends from the fact that Ehala and Pärn are close friends. "We trust each other and know what to expect and it is beneficial to the cooperation," says Ehala, "I can't remember ever having conflicts and have always been included in the process as a collaborator. This applies only to animation; in the case of features, we have had huge conflicts."

Ehala finds it difficult to explain the role of music in film. "Music can provide atmosphere, support the characters or maybe even create contrasts. Good music can also be independent, but the best impression is together with the film. There is a lot of film music you can listen to without the film, but I think the best way is to see it altogether." And if one manages to snag a copy of Ehala's cd collection of film music, then take a listen to the vocal theme from *Breakfast on The Grass*, it is certainly not as powerful nor meaningful without Pärn's images.

Music, for Ehala, is much like animation in the sense that they are both ephemeral. "We fill air with sounds and with animation it is similar. Neither of them gives us any tangible product." And yet both those illusions generate very real emotions from the flesh and blood.

Chapter Ten

Uncorking the Bottle

T here was always some form of Estonian protest taking place during Soviet occupation, but the road to re-independence seems to have found its legs in the early 1980s as Poland's solidarity movement began to gain worldwide attention.

During that time, the Soviet regime was in disarray. After Brezhnev's death in 1982, leadership changed three times (Yuri Andropov and Konstantin Cherenko) in three years until Mikhail Gorbachev became general secretary in 1985.

The Soviet economy was in turmoil and this led, in part, to Gorbachev's famous Perestroika reforms aimed towards restructuring social and economic growth. Gorbachev's proposed reforms would, in just six years, dramatically alter the layout of the world.

The first very loud and visible public display of Estonian dissent happened in 1987 during what had started out as an ecological protest against phosphate mining. From this protest sprouted more active demands for Estonian autonomy within the Soviet Union. But as it became clear (thanks to the fall of communist governments in Hungary, Poland and Czechoslovakia in 1989–90) that the very existence of the Soviet Union was in jeopardy, calls for autonomy soon turned to calls for full Estonian independence. And to make a long, complicated, and at times, dull, story short, in 1991 Estonians had their wish. Amazingly, Estonia's (unlike their Baltic neighbours in Latvia and Lithuania) final steps towards re-independence were accomplished without bloodshed.

While Estonia did not officially become an independent country until 20 August 1991, film censorship had stopped around 1988 when the Supreme Council of the Estonian SSR transferred all cultural dealings to a newly formed Cultural Committee. The state censorship office, Glavlit, then vanished in 1990. From

1992–1995, culture was the preserve of the Ministry of Culture and Education, and in 1993, it decided to replace institutional funding (e.g. Tallinnfilm continued to receive support until this time) with project funding.

Project applications were now submitted to a committee of filmmakers established by the Ministry of Culture. For the first time, filmmakers themselves were making decisions pertaining to Estonian film financing.

In 1996, the Ministry was divided into the two branches of culture and education and a Cultural Endowment fund was re-established (it had existed in pre-War Estonia). The fund was split into eight categories and film was included under the audio-visual heading. In just over a year, Estonian films received more than twice the support than during the previous year.

In 1997, the Estonian government established the Estonian Film Foundation (EFF). Operating under the control of the Ministry of Culture, the EFF mandate was to "advance and support the national film culture." The EFF was also given all remaining Tallinnfilm assets.

When Tallinnfilm stopped receiving funding in 1994, the Nukufilm and Joonisfilm divisions were re-established as independent studios under the control of their animators and producers. Joonisfilm, now owned by animators Priit Pärn, Janno Põldma, Heiki Ernits and Mati Kütt, along with producer Kalev Tamm, became Eesti Joonisfilm, while Nukufilm re-opened under the charge of producer Arvo Nuut and animators Rao Heidmets, Hardi Volmer and Riho Unt.

"We began to wonder what would happen to Nukufilm and what we should do," says Arvo Nuut, "I had a lot of energy and started to suggest that we should get some money and continue to work as a private company. I had made over seventy films and maybe I'd reached a point where I was a bit bored with it." Nuut embraced his new challenge: taking over as the producer and administrator of the 'new' Nukufilm.

What is most remarkable about this scenario is that, with the exception of Rein Raamat, whose Studio B came and went, the animators remained united through this uncertain transition period. As Rao Heidmets points out, it would have been quite easy and more economical for an animator to create his own studio: "If I separate from the puppet studio and start my own office, I can submit my storyboard to the funding commission and get a great deal of money. I could get maybe half a million of the two million that the puppet studio receives and live quite well with this money. And then at the end of year, I can shoot some stupid

Following pages:

Left, Mati Kütt;

Right, Mati Kütt, *Little Lilly*, 1995.

thing and say that this is my project, (but) we don't do these kinds of things." Well ... as we shall see in the next chapter, Estonians *do* do those kinds of things.

Despite a strong alliance among the animation community, the transition has had its setbacks. The studios, freed of Soviet censors, were forced to address a new foe: the global marketplace. To fund their independent films, the studios, notably Joonisfilm, have turned towards commercial and television production.

Estonian independence also meant no more worrying about which Soviet party member didn't like your face or whether Rein Raamat liked you. Three men in particular were prevented, for very different reasons, from becoming film directors during Soviet time: Janno Põldma, Heiki Ernits and Mati Kütt.

While Ernits did have the opportunity to make children's films during Soviet time, he was not to make his first personal film until 1991 (ironically, the appropriately titled *Departure* was also the last film funded by Moscow). Kütt had worked closely with Avo Paistik, but had never won Raamat's favour. Põldma started as a cameraman at Joonisfilm and remained so. "Maybe it's my personal opinion," says Põldma, "but Raamat just didn't see other people as developing. He saw people as final: they are like that and will stay like that. It was like this not only with myself, but with others as well – like Mati Kütt. Raamat didn't understand that we were developing personalities." And it was not until the late 1980s/early 1990s that these three artists would emerge as unique and important contributors to contemporary animation.

Mati Kütt

Mati Kütt was born in Tallinn in 1947. His father worked for a transportation company in Viljandi and his mother was a housewife. As a boy Kütt studied art for a year in Viljandi: "Mother supported the idea and I remember a smock was sewn for me and paints were bought, but as other boys did more realistic things, I quit after a year." Kütt finished secondary school in Viljandi and then went to the Technical University where he stayed for four years, until 1968. "Young children are asked what they want to be," says Kütt, "and I always wanted to be an artist. But, as my grandfather and father had real jobs, I followed their wishes and instead went to university to become an engineer. But I didn't like it and left university."

In 1974, Kütt learned that Rein Raamat was having a competition to find animators. "Rein Radme, whom I knew from the university and was a book illustrator, and I discussed the competition and applied even though we didn't think we would be accepted.

But we were picked. I still don't understand why because my drawing ability was quite weak," says Kütt.

With new directors needed and extra money available, Joonisfilm assigned three directors to make episodes for the short film *1+1+1* (1981). Kütt's contribution was *Monument*, about a man who has the overwhelming task of carrying gigantic monuments to their places of display. He becomes so overburdened by the monument's weight and his surroundings that he stumbles and falls; the monument he carries lands on him and he in turn becomes a monument. *Monument* is a fairly lightweight and unremarkable piece about the pressures that we place upon ourselves, but it certainly shows signs of Kütt's later black humour.

Kütt would not make another film for eight years. He spent the rest of the 1980s working primarily as an animator and artist on Avo Paistik's films. His next film was *Labyrinth* (1989). With its frantic and dirty atmosphere – created with a scratch-on-film technique, and populated with feckless characters who run about feverishly, *Labyrinth* (as the title suggests) explores the theme of entrapment and aimlessness in contemporary society.

In 1992, Kütt produced, at Nukufilm, what remains his masterwork: *Sprott võtmas päikest* (Smoked Sprat Baked in The Sun). *Sprat* is a comically surreal opera about a man who lives unhappily under the sea. When he releases a fish he has caught from dry land, the fish grants him three wishes. After a night of contemplation, the man asks for a woman, a big tool (penis), and a minister's portfolio (a cushy government job). *Sprat* is an incredibly unique and beautiful anti-fairy tale. The happiness that the man finds through his wishes is clearly sarcastic, especially when one considers that Kütt has created an inverted world where people live in the water and fish on land. In our world, it takes more than a big dick and a career to find happiness.

Sprat wasn't all that fantastical, as the film also reflected the challenges facing the newly independent nation. For the first time in over fifty years, the Estonian people had their own political representatives. There was now an opportunity to express and act upon one's desires and wishes. But these desires appeared to be as crass and selfish as they were under the other ideological system.

With his next film, *Plekkmäe Liidi* (Little Lilly, 1995), Kütt again creates a tale both comical and philosophical. This time it concerns a little girl, Lilly, who is angered by her father's contradictory nature. He yearns to fly, yet continually kills flies. In protest, she decides to starve herself until she is as small as a fly. The magic of Kütt's films is found in the way they seamlessly weave between dream and reality. The viewer is never certain about what is true

Mati Kütt,
Smoked Sprat Baking in the Sun, 1992.

Mati Kütt,
Underground, 1997.

or false. And this is precisely the point in *Little Lilly*. Too often adults reduce the world to binary opposites instead of allowing their rich, but now dormant, imaginations to evolve and create new and varied possibilities.

Kütt had the idea for *Lilly* as early as 1981, but because of his strained relationship with Raamat, he wasn't able to make the film for about fifteen years. While making *Sprat*, Kütt realized that his daughter was growing up fast. "People started asking me," says Kütt, "'why don't you ever make films for children?' and I thought they were right and I should do something like that."

But *Little Lilly* is not a typical children's film. A common theme in Estonian children's literature, theatre and film is the conflict between the rich imaginations of the young and the increasingly stagnant, matter-of-fact nature of adults. In *Lilly*, for example, the father wants to fly but is unable to see the hypocrisy of his on-going killing of flies.

Little Lilly actually led to some lucrative commercial work. Some Japanese advertisers saw *Lilly*, liked Kütt's style and commissioned four short commercials from him. With one exception, the pieces are conceptually weak, although they remain stylistically interesting.

With *Underground* (1998), Kütt headed into different technical territory combining his oil paint style and pixilation. In the pixilated scenes, we see a young dancer making a series of ordered, carefully structured movements. But under the three dimensional world inhabited by the dancing girl, perhaps orchestrating her movements, is a two-dimensional world (painted and traditionally animated) of randomness and chaos. "It was an absurd enough approach," says Kütt, "but something that was necessary to bring out the desired effect."

Heraclitus's words immediately come to mind: "The cosmos works of harmony and tensions ... From the strain of binding opposites comes harmony." The idea that life is a continuous flow is but one of the themes in *Underground*. There is also that of perception. The two dimensions and their two viewpoints suggest that reality is subjective. One person hears harmony while another hears noise. There is no single eye from which to see, but many, from different perspectives, with different minds, at different times. Nothing is fixed, all is changing. As Aristotle noted in *Poetics*, if I see a blanket, maybe I miss the bed, but if I see the bed, I miss the room. Conversely, if I see a room, perhaps I miss the details within. Everything moves; nothing remains the same.

"It's the tendency," says Kütt, "that as one becomes more experienced and sees more and grows, that one should be able to make more sweeping generalizations, be able to bring aspects of one's life and experience together and mix them, come to some conclusions."

Kütt's most recent film, *Nööbi Odüsseia* (Button's Odyssey, 2002) follows the journey of a button as it travels in search of its place in life. Along the way Button meets a variety of strange characters, becomes separated from his brain and, finally, comes to rest on a scarecrow's coat. The matter of free will and determinism is central to this bizarre tale. Do we determine the course of our life or are we simply unwitting participants led by outside forces? The unpredictable nature of the journey itself that leads up to this moment seems to answer that question. This is an age-old philosophical question, which certainly Kütt poses from the unique position of Estonia. Estonia is now free, but did Estonians really cause their own freedom or was it just the result of a series of outside factors? Is Estonia even really free now? Kütt seems to suggest that Estonia, like Button, remains in search of its function or purpose.

Kütt brings this strange tale to life though a dazzling array of visual images created with oil paint, stop-motion metal figures, cut-out, bits of drawn animation, live-action, and what looks like sand or even coffee animation. Kütt clearly remains at the top of his game, continually producing strikingly original imagery with content that is paradoxically complex and yet fundamentally simple. And like his colleagues, Kütt never lets his work delve too far into heavy-handed pretentiousness. Almost every scene is laced with moments of comic absurdity (e.g. cows performing a pyramid, mundane opera lyrics like "the cow is out of breath") that keep audiences guessing and laughing – once they realize they are actually allowed to laugh!

Kütt had to wait four years to get funding for *Button's Odyssey*. Even then, he was forced, for the first time, to look beyond Nukufilm and Joonisfilm for support. It's not clear what the problem was, but Joonisfilm's explanation is that they had some money left in the budget to make a small film. So Kütt was presented with the opportunity and accepted, but proposed a more ambitious and expensive project. He was asked to create something more in line with the budget, but apparently refused. Kütt's feeling is that the film could easily have been made by Joonisfilm, "but as they are dealing more with real drawn animation and computer graphics, they somehow decided that my mixed technique wouldn't suit them very well. Although a work place was available and no one was using it, evidently there wasn't enough good will on their part." Who knows where the truth lies,

but Kütt certainly possesses an often hard-line and uncompromis-
ing artistic nature. But why should he compromise? Stubbornness
aside, Kütt is easily one of the most interesting and innovative
animation artists in the world. His investigations into the nature
of humanity are tinged with a soulful mix of classical philosophy
and absurdist humour and are enhanced by a consistently interesting, modern stylistic and technical approach that combines
classical painting with pixilation, cut-out and 3D technologies.

Unfortunately, Kütt has not received the same international acclaim as that bestowed upon Priit Pärn. But there are those who'd
argue that Kütt is a more interesting artist than Pärn. Whereas
Pärn has settled into a comfortable graphic style and has influenced a swarm of followers, Kütt's work, while recognizable, is
always changing, always in search of itself. "Of course, I continue
my way. It's normal for an artist to try to find his aesthetic. When
I look at these young animators at Joonisfilm I see that their work
looks so much like Priit Pärn's. This is very sad because they should
be going their own way. It's better. That's just my opinion
though," says Kütt.

"I still don't feel that I know what my personal style is. My opinion
is that an artist should be changing all the time. Otherwise it
becomes boring for you and the audience if you deal with the same
topics all the time. Jüri Arrak, for example, claims he's found his
style or god and closed the door. For me," says Kütt, "this means
stagnation."

For Kütt, making films is 'simply' about living life. "What's the
purpose of making films? What's the meaning of life, I ask? It's
to live. It's how people choose to express themselves. I paint and
make films. Another drives a taxi."

Janno Põldma

Janno Põldma was born in 1950 in Tallinn. His mother was a
housewife initially, but when his father, a high ranking railway
worker, was sent to a Siberian prison camp (he was released when
Stalin died), she took a job at the Pirita cinema on the outskirts
of Tallinn. "I spent a lot of time in the cinema," recalls Poldma,
"and must have seen every movie they showed." During secondary
school, Põldma studied drawing in private classes with Heinz Valk
(the one time Nukufilm director who also taught Avo Paistik).
Outside of drawing, Põldma's teenage years were rough: "Part of
my education was secondary school, the other was the streets."
After school, Põldma found it difficult to get into post-secondary
school. "Twice I tried to go to university, but I wasn't accepted.
I tried to enrol in history and, in Moscow, cinema. I got good

marks on the entrance exams but it was a huge competition. You had to have the absolute highest marks. I was third best due to my grammar mistakes," says Põldma.

Janno Põldma,
Brothers and Sisters,
1991.

With few educational options, Põldma enlisted in the army in 1970: "I was in intelligence in the army and specifically radio." Põldma was posted in Kaliningrad, a very secret place at the time. The lone Estonian in his group, Põldma doesn't look back fondly upon his army days: "I was sick of it and one day when they were asking for someone who could draw, I raised my hand." Põldma then became a part-time artist. To endure his army years, Põldma spent a lot of time drawing. "I drew all sorts of faces and funny things about Soviet life." One day he read a magazine about Tallinnfilm's plan to establish a drawing film studio. "I don't know why, but I immediately realized that I must work there," recalls Põldma.

In December 1972, upon completing his two years of army duty, Põldma immediately went to Tallinnfilm. "When I returned from the army, I called a friend who was working at Tallinnfilm. She introduced me to Raamat. There were only two or three positions available; either as animators or cameraman's assistants." By January 1973, Põldma was a cameraman's assistant at Joonisfilm.

In 1980, Põldma graduated to cameraman with Rein Raamat's *Big Tyll*. "Raamat had intended to use another cameraman," says Põldma, "but, for some reason, they had a falling out. He didn't find anyone else, so he chose me." Surprisingly, given Raamat's serious demeanour, Põldma found him quite open to work with: "To be a cameraman for Paistik meant quite simply changing some sheets and pressing a button, but Raamat was open to creativity."

Põldma also found artistic success outside of animation. During his days as a cameraman, he wrote plays for the Estonian Puppet theatre: "I wrote one play [*The Boy Who Did Not Want to be an Actor*] for which I won a prize. Then I wrote another play [*The Way from Point A to Point B*] and it was successful too. It was always just a hobby with me though." With his work as a cinematographer on many Joonisfilm productions, his secondary career as a playwright, and even a tertiary one as the author of a children's book, Põldma had little time for anything else.

Around 1989, Põldma wrote a script called *Vennad ja Õed* (Brothers and Sisters). He asked colleague Heiki Ernits to direct it, but Ernits was busy with his first personal film, *Departure*. Põldma was mildly pissed off, but shrugged it off and decided to make *Brothers and Sisters* at Nukufilm.

Brothers and Sisters is a visually striking film with a bleached black-and-white look. It features grotesque-looking puppets

Janno Põldma, *On the Possibility of Love*,
1999.

whose features merge those of child and adult. These hybrids live their lives entirely within the confines of a classroom, but rather than acquire knowledge along their journey, they remain primitive and unable to evolve. They are the failed students of life.

To achieve the high contrast look of the film, Põldma used Soviet sound negative tape, which is very sensitive to light: "It meant that I had to use very strong lights, but I also got a strong contrast. I had no idea what I was doing at first."

Following his next puppet film, *Otto elu* (Otto's Life), which recounts a day in the life of a boy who dreams he is a man, Põldma made the acclaimed *Sünnipäev* (Birthday, 1994). For this film, he used cel (i.e. drawn) animation and a series of children's drawings: "Both of my children draw lots of pictures and, for me, children's drawings are very interesting. They are beautiful and strange, with very good ideas buried inside. I collected children's drawings and step-by-step the idea for a film emerged." The result is a frenzied, chaotic, and even comical musing on the absurdity of violence.

Following his collaboration with Priit Pärn on *1895*, Põldma co-directed a number of TV films for children (see Heiki Ernits section below) before returning to personal filmmaking with *Armastuse Võimalikkusest* (On The Possibility of Love, 2000). A fat, wealthy couple and their fat son, drawn in the style of Fernando Botero, live cold lives together. The son is constantly tormenting his parent with his malicious pranks. Meanwhile, the father is obsessed with watching strange creatures through a telescope. And the mother cares for small, gentle bird-like being. Everyone wants to be somewhere else. When the father and mother ride away together on horseback, with their love renewed, the boy is left to care for the birds. He has learned, it seems, that it is possible to love.

Põldma makes the bold suggestion that individuals must follow happiness, whatever its incarnation, and avoid repressing their desires and needs solely because of societal infrastructures. Sometimes the family unit doesn't work. An unloving family is like a time bomb. You never know when it will go off. You never know who will get harmed. A family is whatever it needs to be.

Despite the underlying seriousness, Põldma never allows his work dip into heavy-handed melodrama. Absurd and surreal characters (wheelchair bound frog, banjo- playing rabbit) and scenarios always ensure that the tone remains light. In *Possibility* (reminiscent of the Canadian animation classic, *The Big Snit*, in which a couple's vicious quarrelling overshadows an impending nuclear explosion), a group of strange, rebellious aliens are apparently plotting some sort of invasion, and a strange little man stands on

Janno Põldma, *Birthday*, 1994.

Janno Põldma, Heiki Ernits, *Concert for a Carrot Pie*, 2002.

the kitchen table continually banging his head against a teapot in an attempt to knock it over. Life is always filled with the unexpected.

Heiki Ernits

Heiki Ernits

Today, one of Poldma's frequent collaborators is Heiki Ernits. Ernits was born in Tallinn in 1953. His mother was a schoolteacher outside of Tallinn and his father was an electrician. He studied drawing at the pedagogical institute and was one of the first with a drawing education to join Joonisfilm. Having seen an ad offering jobs at Joonisfilm, Ernits presented his drawings to Rein Raamat and was hired: "Raamat was looking for different artists and for his next film he needed someone who could draw caricatures. Even though I wasn't well known, Raamat figured I was a good find because I hadn't become too developed."

Ernits didn't start at Joonisfilm immediately. "Some time passed before I really started working there. I had a couple of more years of school to complete as well as Russian military service [he was posted in Siberia and was the man who aimed the artillery]." Following his term with the army, Ernits returned to school by day and worked part- time at Joonisfilm by night.

Ernits' first job at Joonisfilm was as an artist's assistant: first on Raamat's *The Field,* and then *Kas on Ikka Rasvane* (Is it Fat Enough, 1978), a moralistic film about a greedy priest. Before working as an artist on *Big Tyll*, Ernits was sent to Moscow to take courses in directing and scriptwriting. "Theoretically speaking it was such a closed group. It was unheard of to just speak up about an idea you had. You had to work your way up. Raamat was very powerful then and could make things happen. The idea was to make me a director. The directing course was a two year course, but I only lasted two months," says Ernits.

It seems Moscow was not too pleased with a caricature that Ernits had drawn for the Estonian Humour magazine, *Pikker*. The cartoon had been created as a reaction to the introduction of a state quality sign (used on meat products, for example) that was being distributed throughout the Soviet Union. Ernits' picture featured a family whose father proudly wore this state sign on his coat. A censor saw the cartoon and was reminded of an old childhood photo of Lenin's. A scandal erupted. "One day I was called to the headmaster," says Ernits, "and he told me that they had received a letter saying that I should be sent back to Estonia." Ernits was slapped with a four-year publication ban. Authorities also tried to get Ernits fired from Joonisfilm. However, the studio

suggested relegating him to directing children's films, where they figured he could do little damage.

Heiki Ernits, *Departure*, 1991.

By the time of the 1980 Olympics in Moscow, times were beginning to change. Party leaders kept dying and soon things were forgotten, like Ernits' misdemeanour. Because of the Olympics, there was more money available to the studios. However, there were not enough directors. So Ernits, along with Mati Kütt and another Joonisfilm animator, Valter Usberg, was asked to contribute an episode to a compilation film cleverly titled, *1+1+1* (1981). Ernit's contribution was a short called *Date*. As a man prepares for a date, he envisions three amazing scenarios that will impress his girl. In the end, all these imaginings are for naught as he realizes that the woman only wants him, not some superhero, spy or rock star. The film is unremarkable but certainly shows that Ernits was a capable director.

Next came a four part series about *Ramses Vembud* (Ramses the Dog, 1985–87) commissioned by Russian Television. Ernits was the director and artist for all the episodes. The stories were based on a book by noted caricaturist Edgar Valter, who also happened to be a major influence on Ernits: "I took a course with Valter on caricature. His education was very important because it led me on the right path. At first, I tried to copy Valter too much ... but, anyway, he was an influential teacher for me."

Ernits first 'real' personal film was *Árasöit* (Departure, 1991). A couple travel by train to an unknown destination (Europe?). Desperately thirsty, the man goes off in search for water. His simple task evolves into a long and frustrating search for water throughout the train, which serves as a microcosm of Europe. Within its compartments, which represent different historical periods, we see different races and classes all trying to fend for themselves. *Departure* poses many questions about the future of Estonia, and specifically what Estonia's role will be in the new Europe. A question that, even a decade later, has perhaps been left unanswered.

"I finished *Departure* when these old communists tried to take over, so I was able to include scenes I wouldn't have before," says Ernits, "If I (had) tried to submit the film earlier, it's quite possible that they would have stopped me from making any more films. But at this point, no one cared." *Departure* was also the last Estonian animation film ever to be submitted to Moscow.

Ernits followed *Departure* with *Jaagup and Death* a poignant Ingmar Bergmanesque tale about a man who manages to convince Death to give him eternal life. However, the man succumbs to misery as the world around him changes dramatically and his

Janno Põldma, Heiki Ernits, *Tom and Fluffi*, 1998.

friends and family die. He finds himself alone and out of sync with the world. Finally, he begs Death to let him die.

Heiki Ernits, Leo Lätti, *Legends of Tallinn*, 1995.

Ernits is perhaps the most conventional director of his generation. His films are competent and professional, drawn in a classical illustration style, and contain familiar narrative structures.

Along with Janno Põldma, Ernits has really become the backbone of Joonisfilm, ensuring the balance between commercial and personal work necessary for the studio's survival. "At first, making children's films was supposed to be a punishment," laughs Ernits, "Maybe I took it too seriously because I am still making children's films!"

During the last six or seven years, Põldma and Ernits have become a formidable production team, responsible for a series of successful children's tales (*Tom and Fluffy*, *Lotte* and most recently, the Christmas feature *Ladybird's Christmas)* that have injected some much needed income into Joonisfilm.

All three are anthropomorphic tales involving a variety of dogs and insects. Simple though they are, the stories are well realised. *Tom and Fluffy (1997)*, based on Põldma's puppet play *Dog's Wedding*, follows the adventures of the inhabitants of a small seaside village. *Lotte (1999)* is a sequel of sorts, this time focusing on a young girl dog named Lotte who lives in the same seaside village.

Both *Tom and Fluffy* and, especially, *Lotte* were successes internationally. *Lotte* was sold to twenty countries including Germany, France, Italy, China, and Australia. The response at home was just as positive from both a popular and critical perspective. The *Lotte* and *Tom and Fluffy* videos have sold more than any other Estonian films. You can even buy *Lotte* ice cream. *Lotte* also won two major cinema prizes in Estonia: Best Estonian film of 2000, and the Film Critic's Prize.

With the sales of *Lotte*, Põldma and Ernits funded their net project, the Christmas special *Lepatriinude Jõulud* (Ladybird's Christmas) which they hoped would generate further revenue for Joonisfilm. In the film, two ladybirds find themselves in a human house when their tree is removed from the forest to be used as a Christmas tree. The ladybirds spend the rest of the film trying to find their way home via an odd assortment of insects living in the house.

Ladybird turned out to be a phenomenal success, breaking box-office records in Estonian cinemas in 2002. The film was also released on video and turned into a children's book. Joonisfilm even licensed the use of some of its characters for a cola drink, and

Heiki Ernits, Janno Põldma, *Lotte*, 2000.

Estonia Theatre is interested in producing a musical based on the film.

Certainly the domestic success of *Ladybird* can be attributed to a desire for original Estonian stories. In Estonia, as elsewhere, much of the television and cinema material is foreign. Furthermore, while the 'festival' animation films have been successful internationally, only a very small audience in Estonia actually sees them. In Estonia, as elsewhere, 'art' animation has limited popular appeal.

But, frankly, much of their success is due to the very simple fact that the films are well made. Põldma and Ernits approach their children's films with the same passion and seriousness that they would their own personal films. "Of course we were worried about selling our films," says Põldma, "but we tried first to make films which were interesting to us."

Like the children's work of Tuganov, Pars and the others that came before, Ernits and Põldma demonstrate a respect for children. Their films are free of violence and smart-ass kids, and, most significantly, they never belittle child viewers. In many cases, the narration is minimal, thereby allowing the images (the character designs in *Ladybird* are especially original) and the imaginations of children to fill in the gaps.

Põldma was not surprised by the lack of sales in North America. "A friend of mine showed *Lotte* to someone he knew at Dreamworks. They said it was a nice film but that Americans prefer films with heavy dialogue and lots of action. For European kids, *Lotte* is like a bedtime story, but for American children, a bedtime story is something like *Spiderman*. I realized then the difference between European and American cultures."

Põldma and Ernits recently completed *Concert for Carrotpie*. Because of the disagreement with fellow animator Mati Kütt over *Button's Odyssey*, Joonisfilm was faced with a production void and had to rush to create another film. "We had planned for Mati's film," says Põldma, "so we had to work fast to create a script to fill that gap. And everyone else was busy." *Concert for Carrotpie* is aimed at children and its construction is unique in the way its story evolves from a musical concert (composed by Olav Ehala). The basic narrative follows a grandfather and granddaughter as they search for the grandmother who has disappeared from home. A variety of characters populate the journey including some familiar (design-wise) ladybugs and a rabbit whose main desire in life is to wish everyone a good morning. As the story unfolds, a musical band and its conductor occasionally appear on screen to introduce a piece of music they will then perform. The musical styles are

quite diverse ranging from Celtic to jazz and even some bossa nova.

Concert for Carrotpie is beautifully designed, mixing Heiki Ernits' subdued 'earthy' tones from *Lotte* and *Tom and Fluffy* with the more vibrant colours of *Ladybird's Christmas*. As with the earlier works, *Carrotpie* impresses with its simplicity and its understated stories. We meet simple characters leading simple lives where the unexpected sometimes happens. No politically correct morality lessons found here, nor product placements – just a glimpse into a life in process.

In typical Estonian fashion, *Carrotpie* (like *Lotte, Ladybird* and *Tom and Fluffy*) is filled with an assortment of strange characters and actions that would be called surreal if they were found in an adult film (e.g. when the sun comes out of a door to take over the moon's shift). Here, they are merely surprises within the normal course of life. Perhaps it is in these children's films that the core of Estonian animation is to be discovered. What we call surreal or absurd or bizarre might in fact be quite natural and, in a sense, innocent (e.g. What is so strange really about a person who simply wishes to say good morning to everyone?) Children say and imagine some of the most seemingly bizarre things. Although there often is an internal logic to their words, it's the struggle with words and their meanings that confuse – or strike as imaginative – the adult listener.

In a sense, some of the Estonian work of the Priit Pärn era is similar. This isn't to say that Pärn and company are naïve and child-like, but rather that their way of perceiving and articulating the world, which is closely bound with a language that is spoken by so few, is different from 'ours' (from my Western English perspective). When Estonians speak (and remember there is no gender separation) they use a language that is centuries old, a language and a people so rooted to the native landscape. Westerners, with our heavy case of historical amnesia and ease with Orwellian double-speak, are perhaps not fully capable of appreciating, let alone understanding, the refreshing, unfiltered nature of Estonian language and thought.

The success, fiscally speaking, of Põldma and Ernits' works has opened up new and much needed channels of funding for Joonisfilm. The revenue generated from foreign sales purchases new equipment and finances independent productions. The success of their three projects also proves that quality children's programmes can be artistically satisfying and financially viable.

A. Film Estonia

With the new marketplace in Estonia also came new competition. Aside from Raamat's failed Studio B, Denmark's A. Film A/S established a division in Tallinn in 1994. The roots of A. Film Estonia date back to 1990 when two former Tallinnfilm and Studio B animators, Ando Tammik and Meelis Arulepp were hired by the Danish studio. In 1994, the two men convinced the A. Film owners to open a branch in Tallinn. Initially it was hoped that a partnership could be formed with Joonisfilm, but when that proved impossible, Tammik and Arulepp were sent to Tallinn to start A. Film Estonia.

As the studio was faced with a lack of classically trained animators, the first order of business at the newly established A. Film Estonia was training. The studio's main activity is providing service work for features, TV series and commercials. In 2001, A. Film started development of its own TV project, *If I Were a Grown Up*. The series will be co-produced with the Irish studio, Magma. The title sequence for the series, *Film Freak* was selected for the 1999 Annecy Animation festival. Most recently, the studio produced two animated 'postcards' for the 2002 Eurovision Song Contest, which was held in Tallinn. Depending on the project, the studio employs between 20–25 artists.

The studio has also tried its hand at short film – unsuccessfully. *Film Fly* originally began as an animated title sequence for *Film Freak* and was to be developed into a TV series. When financing proved difficult to secure, *Film Fly* was reconceived as a short film. Unfortunately, the Estonian Film Foundation did not support the project and *Film Fly* is now on hold.

Because A. Film Estonia is foreign-owned, Estonian state funding was unavailable (however, the studio was able to access funding if they collaborated with an Estonian company). But as of May 2002, the Estonian Film Foundation's guidelines permit all companies to apply for support. Consequently, A. Film Estonia could provide competition for the small pot of money that currently exists in Estonian animation. If their projects are good, then why not?

Given the woeful state and quality of production in other ex-Soviet-occupied countries, the Estonian story is an unqualified success. Not only has independent animation production continued, but so too the same high level of quality (as evidenced by the numerous awards and prizes laurelled upon the work over the last decade) seen during Soviet times. Furthermore, given the total lack of business experience, the Estonians, especially at Joonisfilm, have shown a remarkable flexibility in adapting to the capitalist system. This should not really be surprising given Estonia's history. Estonia has always had the characteristics of a European country. During the Soviet period, the standard of living was generally better than in any other republic and Estonians certainly got away with more.

However, it hasn't been all champagne and caviar. Estonia has suffered through much economic uncertainty. Most visitors to Estonia rarely see beyond the increasingly cosmopolitan realm of Tallinn, where everything seems fine: a bustle of activity ranging from the thriving nightlife, galleries and tourist sites to the healthy shopping crowds in old Tallinn and the large malls. But what we don't see are the increasing division between rich and poor, the increasing crime (albeit the crime level is actually low compared to most US cities), the prostitution and the not-so-quiet presence of criminal organizations.

Naïve Westerners might believe that Estonians (and of ex-Soviet occupied realms) would just be thankful to have freedom, but that view is faulty. Certainly there is a different form of freedom, but is there more freedom? Now you can fly anywhere, if you have the money. Now there is no menacing Russian bureaucracy or censorship, but there are new menacing invaders called multinational corporations and subtler forms of censorship. One look at the stifling homogenizing influence of 'global culture' clearly shows that differences of opinion are still not entirely encouraged or welcomed. And now Estonia is doing all it can, it seems, to win the favour of the European Union. But as Riho Unt's *Back to Europe* suggests, what is the difference between this Union and the Soviet Union? Are not Estonia's culture, language and resources prey to assimilation? And yet Estonia is not alone in this fate. Many nations are increasingly facing a new form of invasion that comes not through tanks and bombs (although we all know that that still exists), but through culture and economics.

For the most part, Estonian animators offer a quite balanced appraisal when asked about living and working through two political systems:

> "I have to say that the beginning of independence was a really hard time economically for everyone," says Hardi Volmer, "It's complicated still because this period of changing systems is still going on and that's hard. Mostly it's nasty in a political and economic way."

"The main problem is the way of thinking today," says Riho Unt, "The transition between systems is what we can call a time lag. In the previous period we were pushed to think and go in depth more, but I've noticed that we (and I) are not pulling our brains together as much… not pushing ourselves as much. On the other hand, the Soviet films were full of depression and frustration. So maybe we've achieved a balance now. Gaining independence was like uncorking a bottle so we could let out our senses of humour."

"In Soviet time, there was no lack of topics," says Arvo Nuut, "You just needed to capture them, put them into a form and get them through the authorities. Everything had to be hidden and this was fascinating because when someone asked you about your work you could lie. With independence we can talk about anything and some artists didn't know what to say anymore. But now after some years things have somehow settled down. Artists are once again looking at human relations and general themes. Life is developing again."

Mati Kütt claims that there is little difference working in the Soviet time compared to today: "the artist is always in opposition and you have to fight for your place and your money with every regime. In Soviet time, when you didn't belong to Raamat's good boy's circle, it wasn't easy to get money. Nowadays, it isn't easy to get money. Raamat used to make those decisions about who became a director. But I can't get money today. Maybe it's because I'm not a good artist!"

We can't compare the two periods," offers Jaan Ruus, "They are two different worlds, with a million different levels. For example, Pärn and I met a film director from Finland who said that he did not have money to make his film. Pärn said, 'I have enough money to make my film but I can't deal with it because I have to drive around town to find meat to feed my family.' The pressure that was imposed on an individual in those days is gone and people have many more interests nowadays. But in those days we had enough money and we did something."

Chapter Eleven

The Next Wave

As with earlier generations, one of the biggest worries in the 1990s, aside from funding, was the lack of young animators to carry the mantle into the next generation. Obviously, when you are a country of 1.4 million that has just re-established independence, there are a lot of new freedoms and opportunities. As such, the animation studios were not only competing for money, but also for talent (as witnessed with the problems facing Studio B). Ironically, one of the reasons Estonian animation was so successful might also be the factor that hurt its early ability to find new animators: oral tradition. Each generation has simply passed on its knowledge to the next. There was no formal education; one learned by doing. At the same time, this has perhaps intimidated outsiders because almost every Estonian animator had had a contact in one of the studios. So unless you knew someone who knew someone who worked at the studio, it wasn't so easy to gain entry. That's not to say that Estonian animation is a private club; it isn't. Many foreign students, eager to expand their knowledge or just gain work experience, have been welcomed at both studios.

Fuelling the problem of recruitment is the lack of formal animation education in Estonia. Many students might have been interested in animation, but until 1994, it was impossible to study. Even in 1994, the situation was improved only slightly. Priit Pärn was hired to head the newly created animation department at the then Turku Polytechnical School (now Turku Arts Academy) in Turku, Finland (about 4–6 hours by boat and bus from Tallinn). In some ways, it's quite absurd that Estonia's most prominent animator had to travel abroad to teach, but Pärn, very much aware of the future of Estonian animation, stated his conditions: "I agreed to take the job on the condition that two Estonians be accepted without competition. Unfortunately, we found just one suitable Estonian at the time: Ülo Pikkov."

Ülo Pikkov, *Bermuda*, 1998.

Since about 1998, Riho Unt and Hardi Volmer have been teaching at the Estonian Academy of Arts in Tallinn. "There is a department called Cineography," says Unt, "It's more to do with theatre. My namesake, Vilve Unt, proposed to include puppet scenes because of the similarity between the two and apparently now there will be an animation department." The Academy already provides a good opportunity for students to make low budget digital films, so over the next few years we should be seeing more and more new faces emerging from the school.

While there are and have been a number of scattered voices throughout the last decade, there are three animators at the moment who are the most consistently visible and active: Ülo Pikkov, Priit Tender, and Mait Laas.

Ülo Pikkov

Pikkov, who was born in Tallinn, never intended to make animation films. He only became interested in animation after he started his studies at Turku Arts Academy in 1994. "I first applied for some live-action film schools, but didn't get accepted." Grasping that final straw, Pikkov applied to an animation school, just to stay close to the world of film. "It was by chance that I went to Turku. I saw a story in the newspapers about Priit Pärn teaching at Turku and I applied." He was accepted and since then Pikkov's work has received wide acclaim from voices that matter. His student film, *Cappuccino* (1997), played in Zagreb and won a Best Design award at SAFO 97, while *Bermuda* (1998) and *The Headless Horsemen* (2001) were accepted at numerous international festivals and garnered prizes.

Cappuccino is a tale of broken love. A man sits at a desk with a torn photo of the woman who ditched him. At the same time, a nearby mosquito sees his life smashed as the man's hand slams down on Mrs. Mosquito. The two 'men' confront their losses through drastic measures. Given that Pikkov was 19 when he made the film, it contains surprising maturity, a sharp wit, and smooth timing.

His graduation film, *Bermuda,* showed further promise and broke away (just a bit) from his mentor, Priit Pärn. In the middle of a dried-up ocean, a sailor (with a wooden leg of course) lives with a mermaid. She relies on the sailor to bring her water everyday. The sailor, relishing this dominant position, screams daily at the threatening clouds to keep the rain away. Life proceeds as it will until a flute-playing centaur arrives and shifts the balance of power. Through this simple love triangle (Bermuda Triangle), Pikkov suggests that the deafening reverberations of the past hinder attempts at change and the desire to move forward with one's life.

Pikkov's most recent film, *The Headless Horseman* (2001) is his first film for Estonia's Joonisfilm studio. Taking the Headless Horseman myth and the Western genre, as its starting point, this frenetic film (featuring a soundtrack by Sven Grünberg) is loaded with absurd eye candy as Pikkov explores the relationship between the individual and society. A typical western town is calm and ordered. Sure, a shark flies by with a balloon wrapped around his body and cows perform a pyramid, but other than that, it's a pretty normal western town. Unfortunately, the headless horseman just doesn't fit in. Feeling unloved, the horseman and his nose-picking horse wreak havoc on the town. Finally, after virtually destroying the town, the horseman discovers the moon and puts it to use as a head. He's smiling. He's calm. He's still alone. Sometimes things just are.

Ülo Pikkov, *The Headless Horseman*, 2000.

"Maybe the title is bad because everyone thinks of *Sleepy Hollow*," says Pikkov, "but I took the main character because it was just funny and interesting. Someone loses his head and has a horse. He's just like everyone else but he doesn't have a head." Pikkov, always the entrepreneur, was also aware that Tim Burton's *Sleepy Hollow* was being released and he hoped it might provide some additional promotion. It didn't.

Graphically, it is impossible to isolate Pikkov's style, yet one does immediately recognize the simple, but strong, drawing style, complete with bold, almost clashing colours, that is undoubtedly Estonian. There is also that recognizable Estonian thread of the absurd.

Pikkov's films deal with individuals struggling to find their places in society without being assimilated. His characters fear alienation and loneliness, yet reject the sweeping sameness of society. The search for a balance between the individual and community squirms at the core of Pikkov's work.

Some critics have suggested that Pikkov is too strongly influenced by Priit Pärn and Pikkov doesn't deny it. "It would take many hours to talk about Priit's teaching. He has a strong personality and everyone felt his influence. But what can I say? Some seem to think it's his school, but there were other teachers." Besides, Pikkov had no background in animation, Pärn was his first teacher, and he's only 25. With each subsequent film Pikkov is clearly moving further away from the obvious Pärn drawing influence.

His next project, *Year of the Monkey,* draws again on the theme of the individual and society. The film is about a monkey who shaves off his fur in order to become human. He finds domestic and material bliss but decides one day he to escape from it all and move

back to the jungle. "It's actually a little bit autobiographical," says   Mait Laas.
Pikkov.

Aside from *Year of the Monkey*, Pikkov recently directed the Priit
Pärn-scripted television pilot, *Frank and Wendy*. As for the future,
Pikkov is quite uncertain. "I am a realist. I see that I can't draw.
I have not found my confidence yet." Perhaps this is why Pikkov
has enrolled in law school.

Pikkov is doing just fine for someone who supposedly can't draw
and has no confidence. Despite his insecurities, clearly there are
many who think he can draw. Not only is he able to make a living
as an independent animator (and win wide acclaim for his work),
he has also contributed illustrations to books and websites.

Mait Laas

"For me, it's stupid to talk about yourself," says Mait Laas (who
proceeds to do so anyway), "I was happy to grow up with my
parents because they took very good care of me. I was their second
child. The first one unfortunately died and I think they took extra
care of me after that." The family was close. They travelled a lot.
Laas' father worked in a factory as an engineer. His job was to
think up new technologies. His mother worked as a civil servant.
Despite the stagnant job, Lass's mother seems to be the root of
her son's artistic aspirations. "She's always looking at the clouds
and she wants to know what we see. She was always thinking
about things in a different way."

"I was really bad at first," notes Laas. I insisted on sports over arts
because I wanted to be like the other boys, but I preferred being
up in the trees with the apples." One day Laas was even beaten
for refusing the write the number six in a normal way.

And, like Heino Pars, Laas wanted to be a beekeeper. "I was sure
I would go to the country and be a beekeeper, but my teacher
said, 'the boys will beat you.' She wanted me to go the art class."
A further problem was that Laas was not a Comsomol (a member
of the Communist Youth Organization that everyone had to
belong to). At the time, everyone had to have a high level of
education and be a Comsomol. Laas's refusal to conform evolved
out of respect for his rebellious grandfather. His grandfather, who
was a wealthy man, had fought with the Germans against the
Russians. For that he was sent, along with his family (including
his newly born daughter, Laas's mother), to Siberia. All but the
grandfather returned. "I was proud of them," says Laas.

At one point, Laas was called before the KGB. They wanted to
set him on the right path with a little show-and-tell about dissi-
dents: "They tried to scare me with pictures of other punks and

how they could be killed or put in prison. They wanted me to be with their church … I wanted to follow my father."

As the 1980s roared on and the Estonian republic became more vocal about re-claiming independence, Laas was one of the many youths swept up by the romantic patriotism of the times: "It was the best time for youth because we had something to believe in."

Laas made out okay. He was part of a semi-professional folk dance troupe and had many opportunities to travel to some interesting places: France, Germany, and Chernobyl. "When I was 14 we went to Chernobyl on some empty train. This was one year after the accident. Everything was empty. It was like Tarkovsky's 'zone' [from his film *Stalker*]." The troupe had been sent there to dance for the workers, to cheer them up. They were only about 40km from the site. "It was a paradox. They would say no you can't go there, but if you don't go there we will stop the folk-dance tours." While Laas escaped harm during his brief visit, an uncle, who lived in Chernobyl, died of radiation poisoning. "He didn't know anything at the time. He just lived there and no one told him anything. He was sent there to work. People were optimistic because they didn't know anything. It was a form of genocide."

Finally, Laas made it to art school. Times had changed, people forgot. Laas studied Art teaching, focusing on general art and a bit of drama. For his graduation project, Laas wanted to use animation because "it mixed all sorts of arts together." He brought a story he'd written to Nukufilm, met with Riho Unt and Hardi Volmer, explained his idea and was shown the camera and told to "go ahead". "I had no idea what I had to do. Someone put film in the camera, Arvo Nuut told me what to do, and I did it and this was my graduation project." The film, called *Ja Õitseski* (And it Bloomed, 1993), was a paint-on-glass piece about seeds that wish to become flowers.

Following his graduation, Laas studied music therapy and then travelled to Vienna where he studied art philosophy and visual media. When Laas returned, he brought a second story to Nukufilm. But before his script was accepted, Laas was called on to help Hardi Volmer with a film called *Keegi Veel* (Somebody Else, 1996): "Hardi had started a film and he was also busy with a feature. He needed some help." It was hard for Laas, who was a little star struck, to work with the well-known Volmer. "I would do these things and then he would come, say little, change everything and go. I didn't know what we were doing really or where we were going. But it was a good starting point for me. I felt a lot of responsibility … I was afraid but he let me do my own things."

Mait Laas, *Daylight*, 1997.

After *Somebody Else*, Laas was given the opportunity to make his own film, *Päevavalgus* (Daylight, 1997). From a technical standpoint, *Daylight* is remarkable. Its mixed-media technique of photocopied heads (which in close-up look like the dirty, grainy expressionist faces of Eisenstein's staircase victims in *Battleship Potemkin*) on 3D wire bodies is eye-catching and innovative. Conceptually, *Daylight* is almost an anomaly for a young artist – it's actually a positive film. There is no loud rebellious scream against society, just an innocent, hippie-induced call for love, light and peace.

The film is set in a neighbourhood block. A group of boys play. They are dark, feckless and full of pent up rage. They destroy for no reason. A boy with a flower and a smile arrives. The cynical boys frown upon him. Meanwhile, in the background, a man and a woman (the boy's parents?) abuse one another with screams and fists. Eventually, light overwhelms the neighbourhood block and brightens life. But is this just the dream of a sick boy in a hospital? The structure is not altogether clear and it hinders a thorough understanding of the film. But what is clear is Laas's criticism of those dark forces of violence, cynicism and anger.

"I'm a positive person, always on the side of sunshine. I don't like these dark people who are always in the dark, living with their computers. I had the feeling that I had to make this film to help these dark people, to give them back the energy that they had lost."

Teekond Nirvaanasse (Way To Nirvana, 2000) is about a young man who rides what appears to be a death train with many elderly passengers, is as visually striking as *Daylight*. The film is filled with a wealth of symbols, which accompany the young man on his quest to find what he has been missing in his life.

Not only was *Nirvana* awarded the prestigious short film award at the Oberhausen festival (which primarily caters to live-action films), it was also shown on Estonian Television prior to a speech by the Estonian Prime Minister.

The synopsis of Laas's new film, *Generatio* (2005) sounds straightforward: "An architect tries to help his wife as she gives birth to their child. As he does he slips into a fantastic journey and experiences all manner of wondrous things between the stars and the sea." As you might expect from the Estonians, things aren't exactly as simple as they appear to be.

Generatio is actually a complex, visually dazzling allegory about history, culture, freedom and the cycles of life. While Laas' use of mixed-media techniques is somewhat new and refreshing for the Estonian animation landscape, his philosophical and ecological

Mait Laas, *Way to Nirvana*, 2000.

concerns point to the past and follow in the footsteps of his predecessors, notably Estonian animators Heino Pars and Mati Kütt.

Generatio was made for a German produced feature film called *Lost and Found*. Laas was one of six Eastern European filmmakers invited to contribute to the film. "I was invited to a meeting with Nikolaj Nikitin, who is the delegate from Berlinale (the one of the biggest film festivals in Europe)," says Laas. At the meeting he asked me if I would be interested in joining the project and doing the animation part of the feature."

Laas was excited by the request and jumped at the opportunity. "It was really surprising for me," says Laas, "that feature film makers were interested in having animation in their world!" Laas was given some guidelines for the project – it had to deal with problems between generations in new societies – but beyond that he was given almost total creative freedom. "The producers and other filmmakers have trusted me," adds Laas, "and I had the possibility to do basically what I had written in my script."

From the beginning, Laas wanted to use a mix of animation techniques in *Generatio*. "The idea," says Laas, "was to have all the techniques in the film because they also represent the different generations. Also, because *Generatio* was split up in short seg-ments for *Lost and Found*, so I felt that it would be smoother technically if I used different styles. Different techniques will build different atmospheres for the viewer. The main idea, though, was to show that even beneath these different forms or clothes, the line in life is the same. I think it's important that we recognize and respect how important that is."

While issues of tradition and history lie at the core of *Generatio*, Laas also addresses complex philosophical and ecological themes. Water plays an essential part of the film. We are made of water. We rely on water to survive. Many philosophers have also sug-gested that water is the key to harmony in life, that our search for our own rhythm and flow in life is deeply connected with the flow of the rivers. "This ecological viewpoint is very important issue as the continuity of the most important values – the life in the earth," says Laas.

On yet another level, Laas also explores the relations between masculinity and feminity, creation and destruction, and our desire to bring these cycles of life into harmony. *Generatio* is filled with a variety of odd characters (men, bees, a cat, matchstick men, a fetus, and a naked woman) that seem completely disconnected, yet in truth they are all connected, all part of the same stream of life. What interests Laas is uncovering this mysterious essence that unites and separates us all. "Nobody knows, for example, exactly about the soul of the bees and how they know to act collectively, it is not pure ratio, nor is it entirely biological, it is something in between and it is mysterious – that is that."

What is even more intriguing about *Generatio* is how Laas' vision and approach speaks to both the future and past of Estonian animation. Laas' refusal to abide by a singular style is far removed from the recognizable style of, for example, Priit Pärn or Riho Unt, and shows a willingness to explore new technologies. However, Laas' interest in philosophical and ecological issues links him to earlier generations of Estonian animation, particularly Mati Kütt (*Underground, Button's Odyssey*) and Heino Pars (*Songs to the Spring, River of Life*). The clothes might be different, but the essence of life remains the same.

Finding answers is not Laas' primary goal as an artist; he is more interested in stimulating his audience. "For me it is actually very important to activate the viewer – to inspire them to feel or think or follow something on their own. Sometimes art makes people very passive, but sometimes active dreams or visions can follow us through life – even when we will never find the dreambook that will explain it in logical way through words."

Engaging viewers has not been an easy task for Laas. His films are complex and somewhat abstract. Audiences – especially in Estonia – have struggled to embrace his films "I don't try to make esoteric films," says Laas. "For me, they are quite clear. I don't like to destroy things. I think it's more interesting to unite. Everything has a connection with something else. I like people to talk and communicate so that we are not alone or separated. This is my basic aim."

Priit Tender

Until the day he found animation, Priit Tender was seduced and swallowed by the lure of sex, drugs and rock and roll. His entire life changed 99 years after the birth of cinema when he discovered animation. Sex was not sex anymore; drugs were not drugs; and rock and roll merely white man's blues. Five years have passed. Little has changed.

Tender graduated as an art teacher from the Tallinn Polytechnic College in 1995 and his first job was as an animator on Priit Pärn and Janno Põldma's *1895* (1995). Since then, Tender has made three drawn films (*Gravitation, Viola,* and *Mont Blanc*) and two puppet films (*The Crow and Mice* and *Fox Woman*) all imbued with those Estonian traditions of a strong graphic style, absurd actions, and symbolism.

Priit Tender.

Following pages.

Left: Pritt Tender, Mikk Rand, *The Crow and Mice*, 1998.

Right upper: Priit Tender, Mikk Rand, *Gravitation*, 1996.

Right lower: Priit Tender, Mikk Rand, *Mont Blanc*, 2001.

In the mid 1990s, Joonisfilm was worried that there were no aspiring directors, so Tender offered his attempt at a script. "I showed it to Priit [Pärn] and he said it was really bad, so I wrote a new one and it was better. I had many talks with Priit about the script but once that was done, I was quite on my own."

Gravitatsioon (Gravitation, 1996) confronts the arrogance and naïveté of youth in its story of a young man determined to fly no matter what the physical laws say. "It was better than I expected but different from what I wanted. The language of animation is so much different than the language of art that I was used too. Nevertheless, *Gravitation* was a success, winning best début film at the Oslo Animation Festival in 1996.

Following *Gravitation*, Tender was invited by Mikk Rand at Nukufilm to collaborate on a cut-out film based on a collection of fairy tales. "I wanted to experience a new technique and was really fascinated by these new possibilities. Cut-out gives you a chance to leave more of your artistic fingerprint because you are making it with your own hand, whereas with drawn, there are many people doing the drawings." The result was *The Crow and Mice* (discussed above).

Viola (1999) echoes the triangle themes of *Bermuda* and Priit Pärn's *Triangle*. Set on an island, a composer, a dancer and a one-handed chair-man come to grips with their respective prisons. "I never write a script. With most of my films I start with some sort of visual image. *Viola* started with character design, first that of the chair-man and then the composer.M-A-N character. I built up a story based on these characters."

Mont Blanc is Tender's strongest work to date. A man wakes up, packs his bags, leaves his family, and heads for the mountain. Using a strong graphic design loaded with symbolism and the comforting sounds of the narrator from Pärn's *1895*, Tender gives us a portrait of those everymen who flee the domestic for higher aspirations only to find that they destroy themselves along the way. In this fleeting world, the human heart and all that it carries stands as the last remaining flower of stability. *Mont Blanc* is truly one of the most magnificent and poetic films of recent years and signals an artist who is finding confidence in his own voice.

Rebasenaine (Fox Woman, 2001), was produced using stop-motion animation at Nukufilm and is a dramatic departure technically and stylistically from his drawn films. *Fox Woman* is based on a Chilean folk tale, in which a fox goes to heaven to visit her uncle, only to be rebuffed. Tender cleverly transforms the standard animal characters from into a variety of American icons: the uncle as an old, dilapidated, Godfather-inspired Mickey Mouse, an Elvis

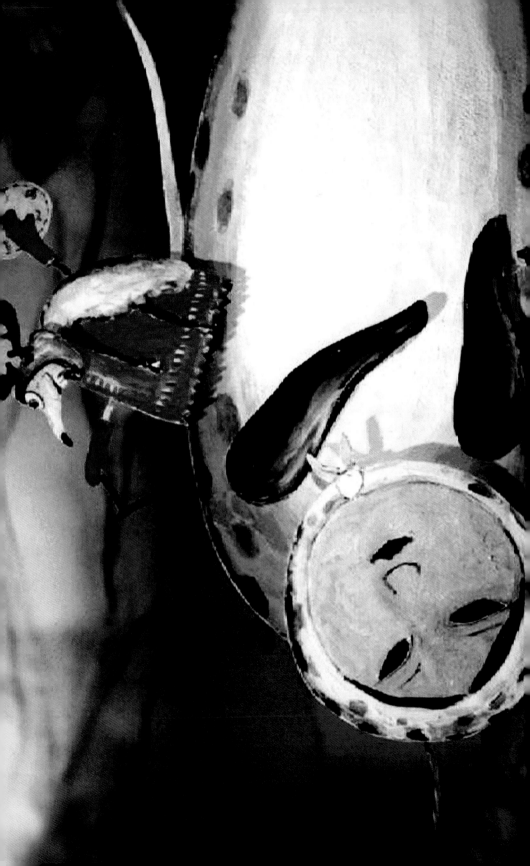

Presley-dressed bird, and the fox as a white trash whore. The film is an interesting experiment and well executed, but the story itself is lightweight and not as interesting as Tender's more 'personal' films.

Priit Tender, *Viola*, 1999.

Tender recently completed, *Sõnum Naabritele* (Message for the Neighbours, 2005). Anti, a TV repairman, lives in an apartment building. One day he decides that he's been fixing the wrong thing. It's the world, not Television, that needs repairs.

The idea to make *Message for the Neighbours* emerged from Tender's need to work on a film alone. "Joonisfilm was making this big children film and all the animators were occupied with that," says Tender. "If I wanted to make my film, I had to make it alone. And the best thing was that I had wanted to make a film alone for a long time. I was really fed up with the industrial way of producing author films here. They are nice people but they make your personal handwriting disappear."

Working alone also dictated that Tender find a less labourious animation technique for the film. "I ended up with ink and brush and not much computer work," says Tender. "I think animation is getting very computerized here and I had a yearning for some real handicraft."

The result is a film that marks an exciting change in Estonian drawn animation history. Tender's raw, minimal black and white drawings break from the Estonian mold and move towards a style of expression that is fresher, fluid, and more abstract. "I did try to move away from an Estonian style," admits Tender. "One strong characteristic of it is the industrial way of production. I dropped that and things did change. The other thing that I wanted to try was the documentary aspect of the story. Most of the characters in my film are based on real persons, my ex-neighbours. Usually our films are much more abstract in that sense. I think our animation needs some new approaches to stay alive and vibrant."

Message for The Neighbours feels like a blast of fresh air on the Estonian animation landscape. Hopefully, Tender's approach will inspire other Estonian animation artists to explore new modes of expression.

In just ten years, Tender has produced a rich and diverse body of work that refutes easy categorization. Unlike many animators, Tender's work has no obvious consistent voice or style.

"I don´t believe in a personal style," says Tender. "As much as I´ve investigated things in life there is no stable ground for one´s personality. It´s just a complex of habits caused by ignorance and

Priit Tender, *Fox Voman*, 2002.

Kaspar Jancis,
Weitzenberg Street,
2002.

fear. We just need permanent self-investigation to get rid of it. My films don´t depend on my personality, they depend on circumstances. If I had to make a film somewhere else it would probably be completely different. I don´t want to make films, I have to make them. It´s survival."

On the Horizon

These three animators are by no means the only young contemporary Estonians making animation films. Kasper Jancis, the second Estonian to graduate from Turku Arts Academy, has made a student film, *Romanss* (Romance, 1999), and most recently, for Joonisfilm, *Weitzenberg Street (2002)*, a comedy about the very strange happenings in two apartments.

Outside of Margit Lillak, Piret Saarepuu, Andres Tenusaar, and Martin Mikson, Jelena Girlin is one of the brightest new voices. Her haunting, atmospheric stop motion films, *Guf (2001)* and *Laud* (The Table, 2004) have garnered international acclaim.

Acknowledgement must also be given to Peep Pedmanson and Leo Lätti, who were Estonian animation's new voices once upon a time. Neither is consistently involved in animation today, but both were quite active in the 1980s and 1990s.

Lätti started at Joonisfilm (Tallinnfilm) in 1982. His first film was the touching *Talvepäev* (Winter Day, 1991). He also co-directed the short *Tallinna Legendid* (Legends of Tallinn, 1993) and was responsible for some of the *Tom and Fluffy* episodes.

Pedmanson, an amusing and highly intelligent character with a fine, dark sense of humour, made a student film, *Kele* (with Russian classmate Mikhail Aldashin, now an internationally known animator) and three films with Joonisfilm: *Reisikiri* (Travelogue, 1989), *Kilpkonnade Lõppmäng (Tortoise's Endgame, 1990)* and *Eesel Heliredelil (A Mule in The Music-Scale, 1993)*.

After living in Finland for three years, Pedmanson returned to Estonia in 1996. When he found no opportunities at Joonisfilm, he went over to Nukufilm and was able to make a cutout film, *Just Märried* (1996). Since then, Pedmanson has been employed in a variety of jobs: journalist, music video director, TV script writer (notably a popular Estonian comedy show, *Vanad ja kobedad* (The Old and Bold)).

Peep Pedmanson,
*A Donkey in the
Music-Scale*, 1993.

Chapter Twelve

Will The Strip Snap?

"Will it go on forever?
Or will the strip snap?
Will the focus shift?"
1895

S o here we are, we've reached the end of this particular story. Estonia, not to mention Estonian animation, continues to be a success story. Certainly the situation is fragile. The more Estonia is integrated into the European Union, the greater the threat to its culture. While the EU will bring many benefits to Estonia, it will also force the doors of competition open wider (there is already a lot of foreign ownership in Estonia). Will foreign studios have access to the film funds? If so, how can Joonisfilm and Nukufilm possibly continue to make the same amount of personal films?

"The issue of the two studios is a serious question," says Jaak Lõhmus of the Estonian Film Foundation, "because we are about to join the EU and the issue of competition comes up and that means you can't harm other people's interests. Other countries have 50 per cent maximum aid but here it is 70 per cent and this means other companies can apply with the same principles." What this means is that previously ineligible studios like A. Film Estonia will now be eligible for the same funding Joonisfilm and Nukufilm receive.

A. Film Estonia might come up with a strong proposal one year that could siphon off funding from the other two studios – funding that both Joonisfilm and Nukufilm require, not only to make films, but to stay alive. This will put, rightly or wrongly, added pressure on Joonisfilm and Nukufilm to find outside sources of income, likely meaning a turn towards increasingly commercial work.

Priit Pärn, Janno Põldma, Olav Ehala, Rao Heidmets and Mati Kütt

The result could lead to the diminishment of Estonia's unique animation culture as the landscape becomes filled with more generic commercial work for television. "The biggest danger today," says Heiki Ernits, "is getting dissolved into this huge kettle where there are thousands of commercially successful films. In Estonia it would prove different if we could survive making artistic films, otherwise the other way will just be to make commercial films like *Ladybird*, and something important will disappear."

EU issues aside, there were and are on-going debates within the Estonian film community between live-action, documentary and animation representatives over the limited pot of State gold. The primary argument launched by live-action and especially documentary filmmakers seems to be that animation receives too much money.

As of 2002, Joonisfilm and Nukufilm were receiving a combined total of about 7 million EEK (about $700,000 Canadian), a paltry sum with which to make animation films.

"We have heard that maybe animation film receives too much support," says Arvo Nuut, "Some consider animation second rate, but outsiders say it's absolutely correct because Estonian film is known largely because of animation."

In 2002, feature film received 16.9 million EEK (about $1.6 million Canadian), a very small amount with which to make films. But the biggest loser has been documentary film, which receives only $4 milion EEK ($400,000 Canadian). While Nuut is absolutely correct that animation is by far the most famous and internationally celebrated of the three film 'genres', all three 'genres' are in fact dramatically under funded.

"There is a problem between documentary and animation because documentary gets so little," says Lõhmus, "The problem is that none of our television studios support documentary or animation for children which would be the absolutely logical to do. The film foundation is in the governing area of the Minister of Culture. For 2002, support was increased by 77 per cent so that it now tallies 35 million EEK, whereas in the three previous years it was 19.4. For the first time it is written into the program that television is going to support feature and documentary film but I am not certain that animation is included in there. The official politics of Estonia since 1992 have been that cinema is a commercial enterprise and that it should cope on its own. But in other European countries almost no one is able to make films without state support."

Depending on whom you talk to within Estonian animation, life is either better than ever, the same, or worse. Typically, there is truth in each view. Joonisfilm is on fairly solid ground, producing

Joonisfilm team of field hockey, 1988.

Nukufilm team of field hockey, 1988.

a good balance of commercial and personal films. Nukufilm has not found commercial success, but nevertheless continues to produce strong award-winning personal films for festivals. Even A. Film Estonia, which marches to a different economic beat than Joonisfilm and Nukufilm, seems to be faring well with service work. However, rumblings seem to be getting louder. Mati Kütt, frustrated by his inability to get work produced at either Nukufilm or Joonisfilm (a studio he co-owns!), found an independent producer to make his film, *Button's Odyssey*.

Kütt's predicament is complicated by the fact that he has no interest in the production aspect of his craft. Kütt has ideas and is loath to compromise them, regardless of economic limitations. And to a degree, Kütt is right. He is a respected, successful artist; the producers should haul ass and find money for his work. They do it for Priit Pärn, so why not for Kütt, whose importance as an artist is equal. Ironically, Kütt showed his muscle in the end by getting his film produced.

Some would like to see Joonisfilm and Nukufilm turned into self-sufficient service studios. This would leave the Estonian Film Foundation's (EFF) money for the encouragement of new projects/talents. "They should loan money to commercial projects," says animator, Mikk Rand, "It's not straight capitalism. The Foundation gives money; the company sells its work. But right now, the money doesn't go back to the Foundation, the company keeps it. This is not a good system. The problem is not with the filmmakers but with the Foundation. Perhaps the Foundation should have a separate pot for artistic and commercial films."

"The Foundation has regulations," says Lõhmus, "and we are not supposed to support commercial productions, but we know that studios need to make TV series. We have supported the pilot episodes so they can distribute them and we also support them to develop international contacts. We have to change these policies because they are not developing the right attitude. It should be that money that comes back from the box office should finance another project but right now the *Ladybird's Christmas* money, for example, is so small that there is not enough there for a project. For now the studios can use it as they wish to."

"To stay alive," says Heiki Ernits, "we need the commercial films but we should only do them as survival dictates. For instance the money made from *Lotte* enabled us to buy computers and do other films on a higher technical level. If we had to reimburse profit back to the Foundation, then we wouldn't be able to do commercial work. There wouldn't be any point in doing it. It would be too risky."

"What does 'commercial' mean?" asks Janno Põldma, "Is *Lotte* commercial? It won Best film from the Estonian film critics last in 2001. Is it commercial or an original film for children? We always try to make good films."

Another problem is the lack of qualified producers who can go to a major industry event and pitch a pilot with the expertise and charm of a girl scout selling cookies. Neither studio currently has a producer with a business degree or command of the English language (a necessity in the global marketplace).

Surprisingly, Nukufilm's producer, Arvo Nuut agrees: "The biggest problem today is the management question and the communication with the outside world, the production/management side. But the hope is there because there are young bright people and we've picked the first fruit already."

"The basic problem," adds animator, Mait Laas, "is that producers don't give us artistic possibilities anymore. You are alone with your own ideas. On one hand it's good, but it's also nice to have some feedback." And certainly in Soviet times, people like Silvia Kiik were more directly involved in a project. But hey, that's freedom and as some guy somewhere once said, 'freedom's a scary concept.'

Another factor, as it is everywhere unless your name is Time Warner or Walt Disney, is distribution and exhibition. At the beginning of the 1990s, there were about 600 cinemas in Estonia and today there are around 70, of which only 20 screens (one of the biggest is the Coca Cola Plaza in Tallinn) operate on a daily basis. Typically, these cinemas are filled with American product. "Cinemas aren't interested in films targeted at students, artists and educated people," says Nuut, "Usually, the authors and studios have to organize their own screenings." And certainly the 2002 success of Joonisfilm's *Ladybird's Christmas* in Estonian cinemas was largely due to its being a Christmas film aimed at families. At the same time, why would a cinema show a Priit Pärn film for nothing when it can fill screen time with a 30 second commercial that brings in a nice cheque?

"There was no audience problem in Soviet days," says Nuut, "When the film was finished it was put in a briefcase, sent to Moscow, watched by a committee, transferred to many copies and then sent around the Soviet Union. There was no problem." In fact, even if the films were shelved, it didn't make a difference, the filmmakers still received their money. These days, if the animators want their film shown, then they have to make the arrangements themselves. Currently the studios give their films to Estonian television for free because they feel an obligation to the Estonian taxpayers. There is also talk of ensuring that every Estonian embassy have a collection of Estonian animation.

"Audience is a problem," adds Riho Unt, "It wasn't so much of a problem in the past because there were fewer options in the Soviet time. Unless you had access to Finnish TV, there was one Estonian channel, a St. Petersburg channel and a Moscow channel. There were not enough media outlets and people were thirsty for information. The films were also shown in cinemas, so there was a large audience."

But there is hope that cinemas can contribute in another way to Estonian cinema. "There is no tax on cinema tickets right now," says Lõhmus, "and perhaps a commercial fund will be set up in the future to fund more commercial works. The official policy is that we have a unified tax system, which means that tax is 18 per cent on every item we sell, including cinema tickets. There is discussion about relegating 3 per cent towards cinema." Of course, this still doesn't solve the problem of finding a viewing audience.

Many of these issues are neither new nor limited to Estonia. Funding, distribution and exhibition issues confront virtually every non-Hollywood nation. Estonia is in a bit of a Catch 22 situation. They certainly have to find a way to bring in money and each studio should work on trying to sell a television series, but there has to be a balance. If Estonian production moves towards more commercial work, it is potentially closing the door on precisely what made it unique and successful in the first place.

"My feeling," says Janno Poldma, "is that [Joonisfilm] must keep the same balance we had over the last year between children's films and festival films. I'm quite optimistic. We have good, young directors here. Our brains are in good condition. To make money you must make short animations all the time and this means our brains must always be working."

"I don't think making commercial films is essential [for Nukufilm] right now," says Unt, "Joonisfilm seems to have chosen a more commercial avenue and evidently they are right. But I'm still following the art path. Without a doubt there should be something that brings in money and part of the studio should do a series for children, while still fostering artistic/festival films. So that would be the ideal situation."

Ideals are always theoretical. Rarely are they found in reality. If Estonia does make a more concerted effort to become a player in the commercial animation world, therein lies the danger of losing the very uniqueness, originality and identity that brought it there.

As mentioned in an earlier chapter, another ongoing concern is the lack of animators. Now with less money available, there is less work. "We're losing animators and cameramen," says Riho Unt, " because of low salaries. That's a potential problem in the future. Others have retired or found jobs abroad. There was a low tide in the mid-1990s, so people just left animation. And we hadn't been teaching young people, so there was a gap."

And certainly it's not a hopeful career when you consider that even studio owners must find other work: "I can't focus only on filmmaking because it's very difficult," says Hardi Volmer, "Sometimes a long time passes between opportunities and you have to do other things. I'm lucky I am educated as a professional stage designer."

There has been talk of establishing an animation school in Tallinn. While there are plenty of teachers, and a sufficient number of students, where are these graduates going to go if there is no animation work in Estonia? Then you face a new problem, as we've seen in Canada: brain drain (as the media calls it). Canadians who found few inspiring work opportunities in Canada headed to the USA for better work and bigger paycheques. As it is, Estonia's most famous animator travels each week to Finland to teach. How many frustrated Estonian animation graduates would end up leaving Estonia in pursuit of a career? An ideal option appears to be some sort of post-graduate session or master's course aimed primarily at foreign students. Naturally, such a course does little for the local student, but it at least serves as a source of revenue, and allows Estonian animators to influence the minds of foreign animators.

Something must also be said about the artistic character of modern Estonian animation, especially that of Joonisfilm. There are people in Estonia and abroad that feel Priit Pärn's influence is too strong. "Artistically, I think there is maybe too much of Priit Pärn and Mati Kütt's influence," says Mait Laas, "On one side it is good that there is a tradition of humour, surrealism, and absurdity, but maybe the young generation is too involved and don't have their own voices. Everyone has their influence but, at some point, you must find your own path."

Certainly Pärn's influence is there. You can see it more overtly in the work of Priit Tender, of Ülo Pikkov and of Kasper Jancis. But Pärn has been their teacher and it is quite natural that they reflect his influence (show me a school that does not possess an influential teacher). Besides, Pikkov and Tender have quickly grown further away from the master's influence with each film, so they are already finding their own voices.

More subtly, the background design and colour in some of the films of Peep Pedmanson (*Donkey in the Music Scale*) and Janno Põldma (*Birthday*, *On the Possibility of Love*), and even in commercial work like *Ladybird's Christmas* show some aspect of Pärn's influence. And without a doubt, there is a Joonisfilm aesthetic that bears some mark of Pärn's design influence.

But we must remember the impact Pärn had when he began making films. "Pärn started a new page," says Pedmanson, "and he did this during Soviet time! He showed young creators that in animated films there are possibilities of doing something in your own way."

"It's not bad," says Leonard Lapin, "It's the problem of a small country. There is one school and in this school there are 100,000 people. We are such a small country that one man is the school. This is easy to see."

There is also the more theoretical issue of the screening context. The people who usually voice these criticisms often only see these films once, within the context of a festival screening. These are rich and often complex films that require repeated viewings to ease oneself comfortably into the film's world. Additionally, the Estonian films are most often seen side by side with different and often more accessible animations offered at festivals. This leaves the film in a precarious position because, more often than not, an audience can't be bothered to accept a challenge from a film. I think that in some cases this has led to the very reactionary and naïve charge that, "oh, this is just a Priit Pärn imitation." Beyond that, some of the backlash can be chalked up to basic jealousy over the international success of Estonian animation.

That's not to say that there are no Pärn imitators out there. Increasingly, there are a number of student films produced in the USA, Austria, Switzerland, Russia, Hungary, etc… that are obvious clones. But this is natural. There are also dozens of Paul Driessen, Brothers Quay, Yuri Norstein, Norman McLaren, Walt Disney, and Chuck Jones clones too.

Perhaps the apparent complexity of Estonian films' often-mischievous symbolism and absurdity have just made them stand out above the many other examples of national schools. If one looks at, for example, the work of the National Film Board of Canada, there are many examples of stylistic similarities over the course of some twenty years. The same can be said of Czech, British, and Australian animation (a majority of Australian films rely on a strong, warm, reminiscing narrator).

And so what does Pärn say to all this? "They are just drops of the same water."

But enough! This is a book celebrating what was and what is, not a tale of speculation and fortune telling. This story is about the survival, expression and success of a national identity and culture conveyed through the medium of animation.

The obvious conclusion to this book is to ask the questions: Why has Estonian Animation thrived? What has made the work so unique? We'll probably never find a single answer telling us why Estonian animation is so unique.

This is a story about different people with different molecules living in different times and spaces making different films with different voices. Even if we focus on one person, we'd never find a straight, easy to read chronological line. Certainly there are a number of converging factors that have contributed to the uniqueness of Estonian animation: geography, Finnish television, caricatures, oral tradition, modern art. But even these don't fully capture the essence.

What attracted me to Estonian animation first and foremost was the humour. I certainly didn't get every bizarre reference, but I don't understand every *Monty Python* sketch either. But it just seemed to me that these films weren't as political, surreal or absurd as everyone deemed them. I actually found them strangely realistic in the sense that they captured the strangeness of life, with its unpredictable and unexplained moments and characters.

Pärn was the first animator to really inject animation with "grim" humour. He managed to make films that depicted the absurdity of Soviet society. Humour became a means of dealing with the unpredictability of the Soviet system. Naturally, the humour was coded so as to be unrecognizable to the Soviet authorities.

But there's also something childlike about the symbolism in the films. The animators seem to have this remarkable ability to capture the world from a child's point of view. It's a view that is innocent, funny, and often downright bizarre. Anyone with children is well aware of the strange words they say and things they do. As the Estonian film critic Jaan Ruus so beautifully put it: "They deal with adults as if they were children and children as if they were adults."

As my interest in Estonian animation grew, I also saw other themes. Here was a small country that managed to make very distinct, national films within not one, but two political systems. We talk today of how much the Estonian animation stands out in the world of animation, but during the Soviet era it stood out just as much, even within the Soviet Union.

Estonians will probably hate to hear this, but I also liked the whole

David and Goliath or "The Little Country That Could" mythology. Here is this relatively small country that has faced incredible obstacles throughout its history and yet managed to hold on very strongly to its national identity. The path to and along independence has been fraught with equal parts ignorance and genius, yet Estonian Animation has managed to do more than just survive; the artists have continued to produce films of the same consistent quality as those of the Soviet era without consistent financial backing. While animation communities in other Soviet-occupied (e.g. Hungary, Poland, Czechoslovakia, and even ironically, Russia) countries virtually collapsed following the dissolution of the Soviet Union, Estonia has managed, for over a decade, to remain a strong and innovative contributor to International animation. This says a lot about the character of the animators (from Tuganov to Rand), of the people and even of the politicians.

In an age when indigenous cultures are increasingly being replaced by a unifyingly sterile, homogenous corporate culture, Estonia's amazing cultural vitality in music, art, literature, film, and animation is astonishing and deserving of protection and encouragement. Many other nations can find hope in Estonia's success and determination.

Select Filmography

Elbert Tuganov

Little Peter's Dream, 1958
Dargon of the North, 1959
Fairy Tale of the Forest, 1960
Murri and Me, 1961
Ott in Outer Space, 1961
A Next to Incredible Story, 1962
Two Stories, 1962
Just So, 1963
Talent, 1963
Good Animals, 1964
Last Chimney Sweep, 1964
Children and Tree, 1965
Mousehunt, 1965
Park, 1966
Stubborness, 1966
Kurepoeg 1967
Birth of Genre, 1967
Cogwheel, 1968
Fips the Monkey, 1968
Donkey, Herring and Witch's Broom, 1969
Atom Boy, 1970
Atom Boy and The Warlords, 1970
Pedestrians, 1971
Drivers, 1972
Nippet,1972
Caution! Cable! 1972
New Friends, 1973
Sisters, 1974
Bloody John, 1974
Inspiration, 1975

Clown and Kroops, 1976
The Golden Donkey, 1976
Souvenir, 1977
The Captain from Kopenick, 1978
Giufa, 1979
The Merchant and the Apes, 1979
The Victim, 1980
The Dappled Colt, 1981

Heino Pars

The Little Motor Scooter, 1962
Cameraman Kops in Mushroom Land, 1964
Jaak and his Robot, 1965
Kops in the Berry Forest, 1965
Kops on an Uninhabited Island, 1966
Johnny's Seven Friends, 1966
The Devil Employs a Farmhand, 1967
Kops in the Land of Stones, 1968
Haughty-Haughty Haughtily, 1969
War of the Birds and Trees, 1970
The Snow Mill, 1970
Insect's Olympics, 1971
Martin's Bread, 1971
Nail, 1972
Pallid 1973
Inhabitants of the Deep, 1973

A Tale about his Royal Highness, 1974
Songs to the Spring, 1975
A Bungler of a Blacksmith, 1976
A Piece of Clay, 1977
Old Mother Kunks, 1977
Old Mother Kunks and Captain Trumm, 1978
Where Men Sing, 1979
Speedy Archer, 1980
Nail 2, 1981
The Town of Honeymakers, 1983
The Laughing Ball, 1984
Seven Devils, 1985
River of Life, 1985
Pea, 1988
Peeping Gnomes, 1990

Kalju Kurepõld

Pine Cone, 1965
Lightning Rod, 1966
Two Heads are Better than One, 1968
The Ram and The Rose, 1982
The Idol, 1983

Ants Kivirähk

The Curious Cameraman, 1971
Those Stories, 1971

Rein Raamat

Waterman, 1972
A Shadow Away, 1972
Flight, 1973
Colourful Bird, 1974
The Gothamites, 1974
A Romper, 1975
A Hunter, 1976
Aerials in Ice, 1977
The Field, 1978
Is it Fat Enough, 1978
Great Toll, 1980
Hell, 1983
The Beggar, 1985
The City, 1988

Avo Paistik

Colour Pencils, 1973
The Star, 1974
Trifle, 1975
The Shot, 1976
Sunday, 1977
Klaabu, 1978
Klaabu, Nipi and The Wicked Fish, 1979
Klaabu in Space, 1981
Three Jolly Fellows, 1984
Jump, 1985
Three Jolly Fellows 2, 1987
Flight, 1988
The Noose, 1989
The Departure, 1990

Priit Pärn

Is the Earth Round?, 1977
And Plays Tricks, 1978
Exercises for an Independent Life, 1980
Triangle, 1982
Time Out, 1984
Breakfast on the Grass, 1988
Switch off the Lights, 1988
Hotel E, 1991
1895, 1995
Deliss, 1995
Absolut Parn, 1996
Free Action, 1996
The Night of the Carrots, 1998
Remix, 1999
Oiva, 2001
Karl and Marilyn, 2003

Aarne Ahi

Nannies, 1975
Does it Move? Yes it Does!, 1977
Goldilock and Rosalind, 1978
A Splash of Water, 1980
The Powerful Crawfish and the Greedy Wife, 1985
A Sweet Planet, 1987
Linnupüüdja, 1988
The House Spirit, 1991

Kaarel Kurismaa

The Brave Tailer, 1982
The Frolicsome Young Tramcar, 1983
A Race, 1984

Rao Heidmets

Pigeon Aunt, 1983
Nuril, 1985
Giraffe, 1986
Serenade, 1987
Papa Carlo Theater, 1988
Noblesse Oblige, 1989
The Gnome's Tree, 1991
Living Room, 1994
Instinct, 2003
Pearl Man, 2005

Kalju Kivi

Sheet of Paper, 1981
Baker and Chimney Sweep, 1982
Knot, 1983
Bride of The Star, 1984
Kaleidoscope, 1985
Why Trees, 1988 (with Toomas Massov)
Rise, 1989
The Goat, 1991
Humachinoid, 1995
The Last Engine, 2000 (with Mikk Rand)

Hardi Volmer

(* with Riho Unt)
A Miraculous Christmas Night, 1984*
Enchanted Island, 1985*
Springfly, 1986*
The War, 1987*
Works and Doings, 1988
Jackpot, 1990*
Incipit Vita Nova, 1992
Twilight Romance, 1994*
Somebody Else, 1996 (with Mait Laas)
Primavera, 1998*
Barbarians, 2003

Riho Unt

(* with Hardi Volmer)
A Miraculous Christmas Night, 1984*
Enchanted Island, 1985*
Springfly, 1986*
The War, 1987*
Education, 1989
Jackpot, 1990*
Schooltime – Geography, 1990
Cabbagehead, 1993
Twilight Romance, 1994
Urpo Turpo (episodes 7–13), 1997 (with Liisa Helminen)
Back to Europe, 1997
Primavera, 1998
Saamuel's Internet, 2000
Having Soul, 2001
The Penguin Parade, 2002 (with Julia Pihlak)
Brother's Bearheart, 2005

Heiki Ernits

Meeting, 1981 (a short story from an animated film "1+1+1")
Kalle and The Monster, 1984
Ramse's Tricks 1–4, 1985–87
Column, 1990
And So in Every Year of Our Lord, 1990 (a short story from an animated film "3 x 1")
Departure, 1991
Jaagup and Death, 1994
Legends of Tallinn, 1995, (with Leo Lätti)
Tom and Fluffy, 1997 (with Janno Põldma)
Lotte, 2000 (with Janno Põldma)
Ladybird's Christmas, 2001 (with Janno Põldma)
Concert for Carrot Pie, 2002 (with Janno Põldma)
Lotte from Gadgetville, 2005 (feature film)

Mati Kütt

Monument, 1981 (from 1+1+1)

Animated Self-Portraits, 1988
Labyrinth, 1989
Smoked Sprat Baking in The
Sun, 1992 (Nukufilm division of
Tallinnfilm)
Little Lilly, 1994
Underground, 1997 (Nukufilm
production)
Button's Odyssey, 2002
Dream Institute, 2005

Janno Põldma

Brothers and Sisters, 1991
(Nukufilm production)
Otto's Life, 1992 (Nukufilm pro-
duction)
Birthday, 1994
1895, 1995 (with Priit Pärn)
Tom and Fluffy, 1997 (with
Heiki Ernits)
On the Possibility of Love, 1999
Lotte, 2000 (with Heiki Ernits)
Ladybird's Christmas, 2001
(with Heiki Ernits)
Concert for Carrot Pie, 2002
(with Heiki Ernits)
Lotte from Gadgetville, 2005

Mait Laas

And it Bloomed, 1993
Somebody Else, 1996
(co-directed with Hardi Volmer)

Daylight, 1997
Way to Nirvana, 2000
The Lightship Kulis, 2001
Miriam, 2002 (TV Pilot)
Generatio, 2005

Ülo Pikkov

Capuccino, 1996
Rumba, 1996
Bermuda, 1998
The Headless Horseman, 2000
Superlove, 2001
Year of the Monkey, 2003
Frank and Wendy, 2003–2005
Taste of Life, 2005

Priit Tender

Gravitation, 1996
The Crow and Mice, 1998 (with
Mikk Rand)
Viola, 1999
Mont Blanc, 2001
Fox Woman, 2002
Frank and Wendy, 2003–2005
Message for the Neighbours,
2005

Kasper Jancis

Romance, 1999
Weitzenberg Street, 2002
Frank and Wendy, 2003–2005